The Big BUT Syndrome®

Presents

How to Get Your Travel Freq On!

While Engaging Your Heart, Mind and Soul

First in a Series of Workbooks and Journals

By

Eddie Conner

Published by Eddie Conner / Soul Awareness
First Edition; First Printing

Design and writing 2016 by Eddie Conner
Layout co-created with Jami Gibson Binding Light Publications

Eddie Conner - All Rights Reserved®
The Big BUT Syndrome - All Rights Reserved®

Soul Awareness / Eddie Conner
3940 Laurel Canyon Blvd #138
Studio City, California   91604

EddieConner.com

Cover Design by Jeff Dannels

All rights reserved. No part of this book may be reproduced or transmitted in any form or by any means, including but not limited to information store and retrieval systems, electronic, mechanical, photocopy, audio recording, video recording, or syndication, etc., without written permission from the copyright holder.

ISBN 978-0-9972600-0-7

I dedicate this book to my beautiful Momma.

You have always been my first
and greatest source of inspiration

I LOVE YOU

CONTENTS

Introduction for the Traveling Soul iv
Using Your Travel Freq Journal v

PURE POSITIVE PREPARATION 1

    Important Information 3

    Packing Checklist 5

    On the Home Front 7

    Touching Base with Your Feelings 9

THE WORKBOOK 15

    How to Use Appreci-Asking 17

    How to Use Ask Better Questions 21

    How to Use Mirror Soul Speak 25

    How to Use Power Word Lullabies 29

    How to Use Projecting Energy 33

    How to Use Sending Light 37

    How to Use Think IT, INK IT 41

    How to Use Work IT Out 45

    How to Use YES-cercising 49

    How to Use ZEN-Tention 53

CONTENTS

YOUR TRAVEL JOURNAL   **57**

    Day One   59

    Day Two   65

    Day Three   71

    Day Four   77

    Day Five   83

    Day Six   89

    Day Seven   95

    Day Eight   101

    Day Nine   107

    Day Ten   113

    Day Eleven   119

    Day Twelve   125

    Day Thirteen   131

    Day Fourteen   137

WELCOME HOME MY FRIEND   **143**

    Welcome Home   145

    Touching Base with Your Feelings *and* More   146

SNEAK PEEK: MEMOIRS OF A SOUTHERN PSYCHIC

Engaging Your Heart, Mind, and Soul

INTRODUCTION: FOR THE TRAVELING SOUL

This journal is designed to help you joyfully blend your heart, mind, and soul's essence together as one. Why? There's an enormous amount of power in harnessing these specific feeling-frequencies.

Did you know that you are living between two worlds? One is the physical world where we can touch, taste, see, hear, and smell things. We have concrete proof the physical world exists because every time we look around, there it is.

At the same time, we also live in an enormous world that governs our every aspect. It's the spiritual world, and child let me tell you, this invisible world is more influential in co-creating our lives than most people know!

Think about it. For every blade of grass, building, or ocean we see with our physical eyes, there are trillions of unseen forces that govern them, including gravity, the spirits of nature, and the law of attraction to name a few.

Since I was a boy growing up in a backwoods trailer park in North Carolina I've seen the *unseen* and felt their invisible influences. As a kid, I assumed everyone else saw ghosts, talked to angels, and had psychic experiences, but they didn't.

As a Soul Intuitive, which is just a fancy pants word for psychic, I've worked with the spiritual realm most of my life. Whether you know it or not, you have always been supported by the Universe, nonphysical beings, energetic influences, and of course, by your own soul!

It's true. We are actually composed of more invisible energy than we can see or hear inside these temporary meat-suit's we live in. By the way, does your meat-suit wiggle and jiggle when you weigh yourself? Mine does too.

How to Get Your Travel Freq On includes Hi-Frequency Travel Tips. Each tip helps bring an intuitive awareness back to your heart, mind, and soul's essence to blend your physical body and environment with your deeper human soul, while traveling through this world.

Here's to Happy Travels,

Eddie

Eddie Conner

USING YOUR TRAVEL FREQ JOURNAL

Why the title, **Get Your Travel Freq On?** Because *Freq* is an abbreviation of the word, *Frequency*. I love acknowledging the power of frequency because it's an invisible energy that can lift our consciousness higher into prosperity, or slam us down into the darkest bowels of poverty.

Who and what decides whether or not we attract lovely things for ourselves?
We do! Who and what decides whether or not we attract challenging things? We do! How?

Simply Stated: Thoughts + Feelings = Reality

There are two frequencies influencing our lives. Hi-frequency and low-frequency.

Hi-Frequencies: Good Thoughts + Feelings = Prosperous Reality

Low-Frequencies: Bad Thoughts + Feelings = Impoverished Reality

Each time we think a thought, we immediately emit an invisible feeling frequency based on that thought. If we think a feel good thought, we emit a feel good feeling which automatically creates a higher frequency. And when we think a bad thought, we emit a bad feeling which automatically creates a lower frequency. Think of it like this:

Hi-Frequency feelings produce rich, happy, prosperous results.

Low-Frequency feelings produce poor, sad, and impoverished results.

Both frequencies are invisible and electromagnetic, and through them we are continuously magnetizing people, places, situations and environments to us in every aspect of our lives, even when we're sleeping! Are you scared yet? Don't be, because I'm sharing my Hi-Frequency Travel Tips to help you magnetize even happier, safer traveling experiences – and beyond!

Now that you understand that every single feel-good thought produces a hi-frequency that magnetizes rich, happy experiences, and that every feel-bad thought produces impoverished experiences, it's time to share how your **Travel Freq Journal** works.

USING YOUR TRAVEL FREQ JOURNAL

You'll be introduced to ten new travel tips designed to integrate your nonphysical and physical aspects as one. I want to pass along these innate attributes so that you have them available to you, whether you're traveling around the world, going to the beach for a day of rest and relaxation, or simply sitting in your own backyard, hearing the birds sing.

I've also sprinkled a few quotes and affirmations that are designed to plant each of your hi-frequency travel tips deeper in your human-soul awareness. In this way you'll be creating your life with the best of both worlds – physical and nonphysical.

I use a lot of terms in this Workbook and Journal. Some of these are terms you may be familiar with. Others come from Eastern Thought and spirituality, like Chakras, which are centers of spiritual power in the human body.

Others are terms of my own making. Bear with me, and if there's anything you don't quite grasp, use your context clues. If you don't get it right away, you eventually will.

I've also provided pages to organize your thoughts, create checklists, track your feelings, list unforgettable experiences, and make other preparations for your upcoming journey.

Whether you're knowledgeable in metaphysics and New Thought or just developing an enthusiasm for this information, "How to Get Your Travel Freq On," conveys some original information and humorous spins to elevate your thoughts, feelings, and frequencies even higher.

> **ZEN-tention:**
>
> My heart's desire with this material is to present upbeat and timeless information to open your heart, soothe your mind, and sing to your soul so that you may create a gorgeous traveling experience.

PURE POSITIVE PREPARATION

Machu Picchu

The Great Wall of China

Chichen Itza

PURE POSITIVE PREPARATION

Peace of mind is a great soul attribute isn't it? A simple way to create more of this hi-frequency feeling is with relaxed preparation. The following pages are provided especially for you to put your thoughts, feelings, concerns, and things-to-do list together in a calm, cool, and organized manner. Enjoy!

IMPORTANT INFORMATION

PACKING CHECKLIST

ON THE HOME FRONT

TOUCHING BASE WITH YOUR FEELINGS
    YOUR HEART
    YOUR MIND
    YOUR SOUL
    YOUR HEART-MIND-SOUL TRINITY

Petra Jordan

IMPORTANT INFORMATION

Driver's License _____
Passport Number _____
Issued by _____

Emergency Contact _____
Relationship _____
Phone # _____
Email _____

Health Insurance _____
Policy # _____
Phone # _____
Email _____

Doctor's Name _____
Phone # _____
Email _____

Blood Type _____

Allergies _____
_____

Achoo!!

IMPORTANT INFORMATION

Travel Insurance _____

Policy # _____

Hotel / Motel _____

Location(s) _____

Airline _____

Tickets _____

Rental Car Company _____

Location(s) _____

Tour Guide Name _____

Company _____

Travel Agency _____

Agent's Name _____

Credit Card _____

If Card is Lost / Stolen Call _____

Alternative Credit Card _____

PACKING CHECKLIST

- ☐ Get Your Travel Freq On Journal
- ☐ Prescription Glasses
- ☐ Prescription Sunglasses
- ☐ Prescription Medicine(s)
- ☐ Camera
- ☐ Computer/Tablet/Kindle/e-Reader
- ☐ Phone(s)
- ☐ Luggage Tags
- ☐ Luggage Locks / Keys
- ☐ Luggage Straps
- ☐ Universal Adapters
- ☐ Jacket(s)
- ☐ Sweater(s)
- ☐ Hat(s)
- ☐ Socks
- ☐ Pants
- ☐ Shorts
- ☐ Underwear
- ☐ Shirts
- ☐ Tee Shirts
- ☐ Dress Clothes
- ☐ Shoes, Sandals
- ☐ Jewelry / Watches
- ☐ Toiletries
- ☐ Shampoo
- ☐ Conditioner
- ☐ Shaving Cream
- ☐ Razors
- ☐ Lotion
- ☐ Deodorant
- ☐ Toothpaste
- ☐ Tooth Brush
- ☐ Floss
- ☐ Lip Balm
- ☐ Mouthwash
- ☐ Q-Tips
- ☐ Make-up
- ☐ Hair Styling Items
- ☐ Vitamins
- ☐ Snacks
- ☐ Bug Spray
- ☐ Repellent Lotion
- ☐ Sunscreen
- ☐ First Aid Kit
- ☐ Condoms, Contraceptives (*wink, wink*)
- ☐ Lube

PACKING CHECKLIST

ON THE HOMEFRONT

What other important things do you want to pull together before embarking on your trip?

- ☐ House Sitter
- ☐ Pet Sitter
- ☐ Water Plants
- ☐ Mail Pick Up / Drop Off
- ☐ USPS Vacation Hold
- ☐ Bills Mailed Out
- ☐ Dry Cleaners
- ☐ Inform Neighbors
- ☐ Let Relatives Know
- ☐ Car Service to the Airport
- ☐ Car Service from the Airport
- ☐ Vaccinations
- ☐ Photo ID
- ☐ Passport
- ☐ Airline Tickets
- ☐ Bus Tickets
- ☐ Train Tickets
- ☐ Itinerary
- ☐ Copy of Travel Docs to a Friend
- ☐ _____
- ☐ _____
- ☐ _____

TOUCHING BASE WITH YOUR FEELINGS

Our emotional energy runs on a scale from 1 to 10, with the number 10 feeling amazingly happy and joyful, the number 5 feeling not good or bad, something I call vanilla, and lastly, the number 1, which means you're feeling heavy, dark or even depressed.

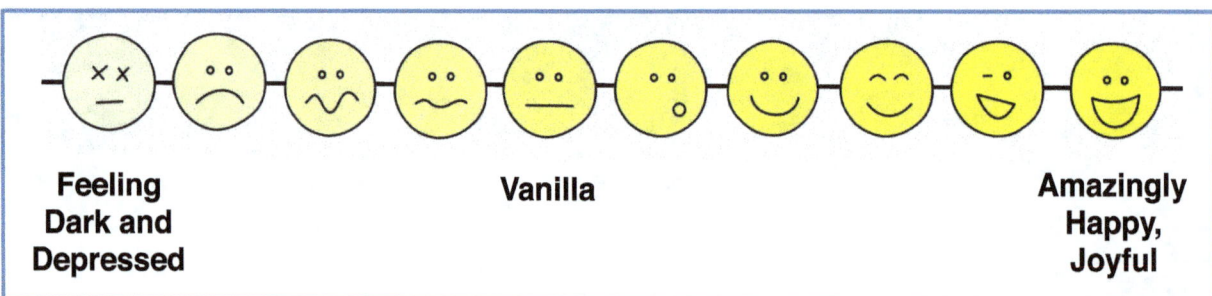

10- Amazingly Happy, Joyful
9- Feeling Especially Great
8- Really, Really Good
7- Really Good
6- Good
5- Vanilla
4- Mildly Irritated
3- Really Bad
2- Feeling Like Crap-ola
1- Feeling Dark and Depressed

Before your trip, answer this question. How do you feel?

CHECK ONE: I feel Good _____   I feel Bad _____   I feel Vanilla _____

If you said, I feel good, how good on a scale from 1 to 10, with 10 being the best?

_____
_____
_____

TOUCHING BASE WITH YOUR FEELINGS

Why do you feel so good? What provoked it? Be as specific as you can?
_____
_____
_____

If you said, I feel bad, how bad on a scale from 1 to 10, with 1 being the worst?
_____
_____
_____

Why do you feel bad? What provoked it? Be as specific as you can?
_____
_____
_____

Using the Energy Scale is a simple way to note how you're actually feeling, versus what you think you're feeling. Many times, we candy coat our true feelings with countless unconscious brain patterns like overthinking, the disease to please, and activity-junkie-itus.

Being busy and moving our bodies while checking things off our to-do list doesn't mean we're conscious of how we feel in our hearts, minds, and souls, it means we're in autopilot mode.

YOUR HEART

As a Soul Intuitive I know that feelings start in our hearts, not our heads. When doing private readings, I don't solely use my brain's thoughts to attune to clients, I use my heart chakra.

All humans come from love first. We are love first and human second. I know in my heart of hearts, whether we're living in our meat-suits or not, we possess the loving attributes of our hearts for all eternity.

While connected to our body, our heart is far more connected to our soul's essence. Our heart connects us to our spiritual nature through empathy, kindness, mercy, compassion, unity, and courage while subconsciously keeping us rooted in the light and love of the spiritual realm.

Over the years, I've learned to rise above my brain's limited abilities and use my heart's heightened feelings in order to receive psychic impulses, images, instincts, beliefs, and energetic patterns for myself and my clients.

Our heart is always communicating with our body and soul, even when our brain is worried about paying the mortgage, or when it's falling into outdated patterns that no longer serve us. Our heart communicates with us through our feelings. It's our job to pay attention to our feelings so our heart can easily guide us in its true language of love.

YOUR MIND

Often we think that creating our realities starts and stops with what happens in our brain. The brain is more than just the engine that drives us. Our brain also is a conduit to a much larger collective consciousness that I call our Universal Mind.

The brain says, "Get up. Go to work. Put in your eight hours." In this section, I am not speaking about the brain so much as I'm referring to our Universal Mind.

Though our brains have thoughts about going to work, it's not the action of going to work that creates our lives. It's our attitude about doing the work. It's our feelings about the job itself, the people there, the commute, how we're treated, and if we're seen in a good light by our superiors. Over time, our habitual beliefs about work and everything associated with it, drops us into subconscious patterns.

We have feel-good thought patterns about work, and we have feel-bad thought patterns about work. The longer we think and live in these patterns the more automatic they become – like second nature.

Our feelings create our realities. How we feel on the inside about a specific subject creates the physical outcomes.

Our brains don't feel emotions in the same way our hearts and souls do. Our hearts and bodies feel things. Yes, our brain thinks thoughts that ultimately cause us to feel hi-frequency happiness, or low-frequency fears, but we choose our thoughts. We have free will to pick good thoughts or bad thoughts. Based on these feeling frequencies, it's we who choose what we think.

It takes a little bit of practice each day to deliberately direct our thoughts and feelings to higher frequencies. Once we do, we can see and feel the power of intentionally harnessing our Universal Mind to create a better life.

YOUR SOUL

Like the Universe, our Soul is unconditional love personified. Our soul is the invisible energy living inside and outside of our physical bodies, eternally guiding and supporting us.

At the end of our lives, when we leave these bodies, we will re-emerge into our Soul's Light. Once there, we will still have many of the focused nonphysical attributes we had while living on Earth.

Once returned to our soul's light, our sincerest thoughts, feelings, and frequencies will remain perfectly intact, as will our imagination, passion, excitement, and unconditional consciousness.

We don't need to have a physical shell to contain these qualities, as these are our Soul's Attributes. Before our birth, as our consciousness came forth from nonphysical reality to live here as human expressions, we had invisible attributes and we'll take these with us when we leave this dimension.

YOUR HEART, MIND, AND SOUL TRINITY

My favorite spiritual teacher, Abraham-Hicks says, "Humans are 99.99% nonphysical energy and only .01% physical. A human's actions and words create less than .01%, while their feelings create 99.99% of their lives!"

Imagine how psyched I was to hear this, and too *feel it* too! Think about how huge that statement is! Our pure flowing, hi-frequency feelings have 99.99% more power to create our realities than our actions and words put together. Crazy right?

The moment I heard this teaching from Abraham-Hicks, it made sense to me, because throughout my life I had secretly worked with my soul, angels, and spirit guides before I had the nerve to tell anyone about them.

I felt Abraham-Hick's words deep within in my heart, mind, and soul. Even today, their teachings raise the hair on my arms and evoke the same inner knowing I had as a kid, when divine intelligence guided me.

We are more than what we see and hear with our eyes and ears! Blood, sweat, and tears are great to gauge our physical expression of emotion, but at the end of the day, we're only .01% closer to having our desired reality, unless we learn to use our feelings to transform these desires into manifestations.

It's been my experience that our heart, mind, and soul each carry different feeling frequencies. We must learn to relax into the unconditional love that composes our heart, mind, and soul. Remember, these aspects of our earthly experiences are already pure, positive energy. All we have to do is tap into them.

Your heart, mind, and soul are absolute consciousness. Even without your physical body, their energies simultaneously live and breathe in our earthly and nonphysical perspectives. Your heart, mind, and soul love you. Pay close attention to them, because they are eternally communicating with you through the invisible language of your thoughts, feelings, and frequencies.

THE WORKBOOK

Machu Picchu

The Great Wall of China

Chichen Itza

THE WORKBOOK

Welcome to the Workbook Section of your Journal. In this segment I'm excited to offer Ten Hi-Frequency Tips that have changed my life in wonderful ways.

As a Soul Intuitive for 25 years, I know firsthand how easy it is for my clients to contradict their desires with habitual, low-frequency thoughts and feelings that extinguish their dreams.

I believe in these essential tips and use them daily. Some are original ideas I've created, and others are staples in metaphysical living. Throughout your journal I'll give brief definitions of each new philosophy, followed by a personal story I've experienced as a result of living hi-frequency principles.

Each Travel Tip segment ends with rich prompts designed to help you experience the world through your heart, your mind, and your soul. As you consciously apply each new philosophy, you'll begin to sense the world with heightened awareness. If you're an empathetic person, you may literally sense and feel the invisible world's influence around you. On that note my friend, let's get started.

INTRODUCING YOUR TEN HI-FREQUENCY TRAVEL TIPS

- **Appreci-Asking**
- **Ask Better Questions**
- **Mirror Soul Speak**
- **Power Word Lullabies**
- **Projecting Energy**
- **Sending Light**
- **Think IT, INK IT**
- **Work IT Out**
- **YES-cercising**
- **ZEN-tention**

How To Use Appreci-Asking

I recognize one of the purest forms of "asking" the universe for what I desire is by consciously appreciating everything in my life. I've combined Appreciation and Asking into one philosophical term, Appreci-Asking®!

Appreci-Asking 1- Bypasses outdated programming.
2- Sends pure energy signals from us to the universe.
3- Benefits us and others in miraculous ways.

For me, Appreci-Asking has been a game changer. It's transformed my traveling experiences in miraculous ways.

Abraham-Hicks says, "Each time we appreciate something, we harmonize with that which we are appreciating." Meaning, if I appreciate a stunning sunset in a gorgeous part of the world, my invisible essence becomes one with the energy of the sunset. In that moment, the sunset and I become one succinct consciousness. The same effect is true with our tangible realities.

When I appreciate the money I currently have, I'm harmonizing with the fundamental nature of "more money." In this way the universe brings more prosperity. I appreciate all kinds of things, and often. This taps me into the positive aspects of people, places, and landscapes in the world around me.

Today while you're out and about in the world, be sure to feel authentic appreciation from your heart for as many things as you can.

Feel the hi-frequency essence of appreciation within you, then state, "Thank you Universe."

Appreci-Asking FROM THE HEART

My happiest moments have always been when my heart, mind, and soul are on the same plane as my brain. A great example is the first time I decided to visit Peru. Instead of telling anyone about my huge desire to travel there, I dove into the deepest reservoirs of appreciation I could muster by cutting pictures from magazines, brochures, and watching Shirley MacLaine's movie, "Out On a Limb."

Once a week I'd playfully spread magazine articles, postcards, and pictures of Peru across my bed and play uplifting music. I'd happily visualize myself hiking in Machu Picchu and petting the alpacas, all while doing my best Shirley MacLaine imitation. After weeks of this, I got a call from a friend in North Carolina asking me if I knew anything about Machu Picchu.

I laughed. "Yes! Why do you ask?"

"Because I want to go," he replied, "But only if I can find a spiritual person to travel with."

I couldn't believe my ears. My heart was pounding out of my chest. Goosebumps covered my neck and arms. Thirty minutes later we hung up, and my first trip to Peru was miraculously locked in, to the exact place I had purely visualized. Did I mention this 10-day trip was an all expenses paid vacation? What the bleep?

Since then, friends have asked, "How the heck did you manifest Peru so fast?"

At the time, I was euphoric about Peru. I held that appreciative euphoria in every cell, atom, and molecule of my being. As I'd gathered my Peru goodies I had also held the holistic feelings of already *being there* in my heart, mind and soul, essentially creating my first trip to Peru, just by having a blast Appreci-Asking.

Today I lead tours around the world, and my favorite spot to visit by far has always been Machu Picchu, Peru!

Appreci-Asking WITH YOUR HEART

Your Heart Chakra is unconditional love. It has the ability to feel the physical and nonphysical worlds simultaneously. When you choose to see the world through the filter of your heart's love, miracles can happen.

What does your heart most appreciate about you? And why?

_____

_____

Appreci-Asking WITH YOUR MIND

Like your heart, the Universal Mind has the ability to move between other dimensions because its frequency is so pure. This isn't about your brain; it's about using the greater consciousness you owned before you chose this physical life.

What does your mind most love about you? And why?

_____

_____

Appreci-Asking WITH YOUR SOUL

Our gorgeous soul is eternal consciousness. It holds the feelings, memories and experiences from every physical and nonphysical life experience we've ever had. It's also pure, positive unconditional love.

What does your soul most love about you? And why?

_____

_____

Appreci-Asking WITH YOUR WHOLE BEING

Ever have one of those days when you were batting a thousand? Everything was perfect and felt great? Chances are, in that moment you were brilliantly operating from the divine power of your heart, mind, and soul all at the same time!

What does your heart, mind, and soul most love about you? And why?

_____
_____
_____
_____
_____
_____
_____
_____
_____
_____

How To Use Ask Better Questions

Asking great questions from our heart-mind stimulates our brain, causing it to fire more powerfully. More often than not, the questions most people ask are stagnant and complacent.

As I've noted before, there are only two frequencies throughout the universe. One frequency is high and the other is low. The Hi-Frequency feels good and promotes prosperity consciousness. The Low-Frequency feels bad and promotes poverty.

Essentially, this means that there are only two types of questions a person asks. The first one is a Hi-Frequency question which promotes prosperity. For example: "I wonder how many gorgeous things I'll see in my travels today?"

Unfortunately, it's more common for people to ask Low-Frequency questions. Low-Frequency questions create the feeling that we are lacking something. Lower frequencies keep us stuck in complacent cycles, making us feel trapped.

A Hi-Frequency Traveler might ask:
What stunning things are waiting to surprise me today?
What else can I do to stay connected to my heart's desire?

A Low-Frequency Traveler might ask:
Could traffic be any worse in this country?
What else could possibly go wrong for me today?

Be playful about asking better questions. It can improve your mind, body, and your life, plus it puts you in a receiving mood and opens you to new possibilities and experiences.

Ask Better Questions FROM THE HEART

When I was a kid, I asked lots of questions. Well, that's not true - I started out asking, then realized being curious was a bad thing at home, school, church, and especially at Grandma's house. My curiosity quickly became taboo; in fact, it was outlawed.

Back then, I wanted to know why bad things happened to good people, and why certain people were happy and others sad. Each inquiry was met with a hard look by Grandma or a pop up-side-the-head, and sometimes both.

At night, after saying prayers, while lying in my bed waiting to fall asleep, I'd ask my angels and spirt guides the same questions the adults didn't have the patience or knowledge to answer.

I learned more talking with my angels each night than I did in years of structured education. I kept this connection until my late teens, then it disappeared, or so I thought. But then, in my twenties, it resurfaced.

My connection to spirit reopened because I was going through personal turmoil, as described in my upcoming memoir, and it was the first time in my adult life that I actively pursued my curiosity about all things psychic, spiritual, and metaphysical.

Deeply curious about why I was living such a hard knocks life, I reverted to asking powerful, burning questions. And you know what? The more questions I got answered, the more curious I became.

My favorite questions are the ones that merge my heart, mind, and soul as one. To this day, some of my favorite questions are:

How many beautiful experiences can I achieve today?
What's the best way to keep my mind and heart open?
How much higher can I raise my frequency while being of service?

As a kid, I got in trouble for asking. Now I know that it set me up to understand the nuts and bolts of the spiritual world that works in harmony with us, if we'll pay attention to it.

Ask Better Questions WITH YOUR HEART

As you tap deeper into your Heart Chakra, you'll begin to sense its unconditional love supporting every aspect of your life. Remember, seeing the world through the filter of your heart's love can shift your soul's perspective and change your life.

What is your heart the most curious about? And why?

_____

_____

Ask Better Questions WITH YOUR MIND

The Universal Mind is expanded consciousness, and has the ability to easily guide us through life. Remember, it isn't about your brain, it's about using the greater consciousness you owned before this lifetime and still possess.

What is it, that your mind regularly asks for, and why?

_____

_____

Ask Better Questions WITH YOUR SOUL

An amazing thing about your soul is that it holds all memories from every physical life we've lived, plus the between-lives we experienced when we didn't have human bodies. It is an unconditionally loving friend, cheerleader, and guide.

Where in life does your soul seem to ask the most questions?

_____

_____

Ask Better Questions WITH YOUR WHOLE BEING

Don't you love days when you feel tuned in, tapped in, and turned on to the pure, positive energy that creates worlds? When we have days like these, it's surely because we're living from our heart, mind, and soul selves!

What is this beautiful trinity asking of you in this moment? And why?

_____
_____
_____
_____
_____
_____
_____
_____
_____
_____

How To Use Mirror Soul Speak

Our eyes are the windows to our soul. Personally, I've discovered that consistently thinking nice things about myself makes it easier when I'm in front of the mirror. Instead of only seeing the crow's feet, (or condor claws), around my eyes, I work at focusing on the positive aspects that make me feel better.

Mirror Soul Speak is about talking directly to our subconscious mind by standing in front of a mirror and looking into our left eye, which is the psychically receptive eye. Imagine you're speaking to your heart's desire and your words are downloaded directly into your subconscious mind. This is not a passive, "I feel attractive today," exercise. It's a direct, intentional conversation you're having in order to reprogram your subconscious mind.

Now that you're in front of the mirror looking into your left eye, speak directly to your subconscious with love. You are giving this aspect of yourself intentional guidance. You're speaking softly from your higher self.

When I began Mirror Soul Speaking, I started my sentences by identifying the old pattern once and then restating the new program three to five times each. My old belief used to be, "I'm nervous about traveling outside the United States."

I've easily replaced that old belief with new, feel-good thoughts. For example:

I love traveling to exotic locations.
I appreciate new cultures and learn great things as a result.
I respect and honor others and they respect and honor me.
International travel stretches my soul.
I am divinely guided, protected and inspired wherever I go, whatever I do.

If you're like me, you're shy in front of a mirror. Remember, you're doing Mirror Soul Speak to uplift yourself and others. The happier you are, the more you're able to contribute to the planet.

This morning and evening, practice Mirror Soul Speaking, simply for the joy of it.

Mirror Soul Speak FROM THE HEART

The first few times I did mirror work, I stood in front of the mirror horrified, wanting to scream, "Mirror, mirror on the wall, I'm flinging your ass down the hall." It's safe to say that many of us have mirror drama.

The great mystic, Osho said, "If you love yourself, you love others. If you hate yourself, you hate others. Because in a relationship with others, the other is nothing but a mirror." This is so true. Every day mirrors reflect our body, while the nonphysical realm mirrors our innermost feelings every second. If we're vibrating negativity, we get negative results. If we're vibrating hi-frequency thoughts and feelings, it reflects back happy physical realities.

Before co-facilitating my first, *"Sail Into Your Soul – A Journey Into Bliss,"* Mexican Riviera Cruise with 85 attendees, I practiced mirror soul speak for a few weeks. Each evening before bed I'd light three candles in my bathroom, one candle each for my heart, mind, and soul. I'd turn off the lights and repeat positive affirmations over and over in the mirror for a few minutes.

I repeated statements that affirmed my heart's desire. Sentences like:

My light and love meet me wherever I travel.
I AM a soul expressing my core essence energy.
I enjoy summoning my personal life force energy.

I did this before going to bed. Once in bed, I continued my repetition so that I'd fall asleep inside the frequency of these affirmations. Often, the way we feel when we fall asleep is also the way we wake up feeling the next morning.

It takes a spiritually centered person to stand in front of a mirror and focus on their positive aspects. We have free will. We can choose the old low-frequency thoughts or we can choose the new hi-frequency desires. It is our choice. I say, don't waste a second of your life; think a beautiful thought right now!

Here's one: "Mirror, mirror within my Soul, thanks for creating me healed and whole."

Mirror Soul Speak WITH YOUR HEART

Your Heart Chakra sees you as healed, whole, and healthy in every aspect of your life. It knows that you chose this lifetime and its lessons, and it supports all of your choices unconditionally, even when you don't.

What is your heart reflecting back to you? And why?

_____

_____

Mirror Soul Speak WITH YOUR MIND

Great ideas often come from our Universal Mind, especially when we're relaxed and chilled out. Each time we appreciate and acknowledge this greater aspect of ourselves, the more aligned we'll become in our bodies, minds, and spirits.

What pure thoughts does your mind want you to focus on?

_____

_____

Mirror Soul Speak WITH YOUR SOUL

The soul is perfection in action. Its nonphysical attributes always keep us steady, on course, and in alignment with our life purpose. Plus, our soul also has a great sense of humor. Did you know that?

What is your soul emanating now? Why?

_____

_____

Mirror Soul Speak WITH YOUR WHOLE BEING

When's the last time you got so excited about something that you ran through your house screaming with joy, happiness, and euphoria? When you had that experience, did you notice how you felt in your heart, mind, and soul?

What does your heart, mind, and soul enjoy doing the most? Why?

_____
_____
_____
_____
_____
_____
_____
_____
_____
_____

How To Use Power Word Lullabies

When getting ready for a good night's sleep, use a Power Word Lullaby. Choose three Power Words to repeat, like a mantra. Power Words feel good to us, especially when our mind and body are slowly moving into a state of slumber.

Pick three words tonight that best describe the essence you want to experience during your vacation. Say these three Power Words in a lulling voice while falling asleep, when waking up in the morning, or during meditative moments throughout your trip.

Here is a small list of Power Words to choose from. Pick three Power Words that are easy to remember, and that feel great repeating.

Sacred	Healing	Spiritual	Successful	Uplifting
Ease	Intuitive	Mystical	Miraculous	Perfect
Excellent	Valuable	Divine	Safe	Soulful

As an example, I've chosen the words: Spiritual, Sacred, and Soulful. I liken lullabies to techniques used by hypnotherapists to take clients deeper into a relaxed space. As we speak in a lulling voice, our conscious mind begins to relax and fall deeper into a restful, receptive place.

Here we go. You're in the bed in a comfortable position, speaking to yourself in a lulling tone. Softly tell your mind you're falling deeper into a relaxed state. By doing this you tell your subconscious mind what to do so that it doesn't focus on worries or negative thoughts. When your breath slows down, and you feel your mind responding to your Power Words, continue speaking in a soft voice, weaving your three Power Words through your now sleepy mind.

Repeat the words…Spiritual…Sacred…Soulful…over and over slowly until you fall fast asleep.

Now, when you fall asleep, your subconscious mind has something Spiritual, Sacred and Soulful to work on for your hi-frequency adventure.

Power Word Lullabies FROM THE HEART

Recently I saw Caesar Milan, The Dog Whisperer, at LAX. He's quick to say, "I don't train dogs; I train humans how to be pack leaders." Caesar teaches owners how to be calm and assertive. Though I don't have a puppy, I thought about focusing this calm, assertive energy with Power Word Lullabies during my trip. The words I had picked were 'cool,' 'calm,' and 'light.'

After completing a 5-day tour in Nashville I boarded my express flight back to Los Angeles, still practicing my three power words. Cool, calm and light.

My seat was in the back of the plane next to the bathroom and it was hot as Hades. Our plane took off. As our flight attendant made her rounds, I pleasantly asked her why it was so much hotter in the back.

She smiled. "It's the engines. It's 20 degrees hotter than in the front, especially during summer."

Instead of feeling crabby and complaining like the other passengers, I remained relaxed, closed my eyes, and recited my power words. Cool, calm and light, over and over to myself. I enjoyed practicing these words. I even reflected on my trip to Alaska years earlier while visualizing the Hubbard Glacier. And just for giggles I imagined I was one of the lucky few who got ice water in hell.

Moments later the flight attendant, Jessica, brought me a cup of ice saying, "This will make you feel better." I smiled, thanked her and continued appreciating my Power Word Lullabies. I was lost in feeling blissful when Jessica returned ten minutes later to say, "The lady in seat 5-A is freezing up front and wanted to know if you would be willing to switch seats with her?"

I said, "Sure, I'd love to."

For the rest of the trip I was in the front of the plane, it was twenty degrees cooler and I continued beaming with gratitude, relishing how amazing life can be when we do the inner work. Especially when we consciously bask in the frequency of calm, cool, and light.

Power Word Lullabies WITH YOUR HEART

Whether you're awake or sleeping, it's your Heart Chakra that sees the world through the filter of love, light, and oneness. Its goal is to help you to see, sense, and feel the world through both your physical and nonphysical senses.

Your heart has a favorite place where it lulls you into relaxation. Where is that place?

_____

_____

Power Word Lullabies WITH YOUR MIND

When you're asleep, your Universal Mind is still awake. It's working unconditionally to bring you new, uplifting ways to interpret the world. When your brain is calm and at peace, it receives messages from this expanded consciousness with greater ease.

How do you feel about the fact that your mind loves you unconditionally?

_____

_____

Power Word Lullabies WITH YOUR SOUL

You recognize that your soul, like your heart and mind, is pure, positive unconditional love. It works to keep you centered and in sync with your greater good. Being aware of this fact is enough to shift your thoughts higher and higher.

Write three spiritually charged words that make you smile. Why do you like them?

_____

_____

Power Word Lullabies WITH YOUR WHOLE BEING

Go back in time to when you were a kid, playing. Remember how easy it was to relax into coloring, climbing trees, pretending, and daydreaming? That's just another example of your connection to your heart, mind, and soul.

Can you define the frequency of the words, 'Heart,' 'Mind,' and 'Soul?'

_____
_____
_____
_____
_____
_____
_____
_____
_____
_____

How To Use Projecting Energy

Before I start a new project, or head out on tour to promote hi-frequency living techniques, I often ask, "Which arrives to my destination first, my thoughts and feelings about my trip, or my physical body?"

My thoughts and feelings arrive at my destination long before I leave the house. My energy shows up before my physical self does, so I quickly toss my low-frequency nervousness out the back door and begin deliberately creating a mental or written outline to enhance my upcoming projects. I consciously feel good while writing my ideal end results. This makes me the intentional captain of my ship instead of a victim of circumstances. This is true for everyone in every aspect of life.

What kind of energetic frequency have you projected to prepare for your trip? Was it a frequency of ease, flow, and well being or a low-frequency energy of exhaustion, irritation or fear? If you've projected the latter, please don't worry. It's not too late to easily shift your thoughts and feelings. Here's how:

Spend two minutes an hour reestablishing your thoughts and feelings to reflect on what you Do Want instead of what you Don't Want. If you embarked on your trip feeling nervous or anxious, focus on feeling calm, relaxed and reassured. Spend as much time observing all the calm, relaxing, or reassuring things around you. You will begin to feel your former anxious energy melt away as your new hi-frequency energy takes hold!

The next time you have a negative feeling about a trip, experience, or event that's important to you, ask yourself, "Do I want the frequency from my negative thoughts and feelings to meet me again in the immediate future?" If you answer 'no,' remember to shift your low-frequency into your desired energy so that you attract and create the best experience ever.

Projecting Energy FROM THE HEART

When traveling on business to North Carolina, my first stop was always at my Momma's to spend time with her. On this particular visit I lost my business checkbook and realized this, hours before my return flight to Los Angeles.

I remained calm. While dismantling my luggage, I reminded myself that for this trip, I'd already projected the energy of 'all is well.' While combing through every inch of my bedroom, rental car, and Momma's home, I mentally backtracked to every place I'd been that week. Still no luck finding my checkbook.

The clock ticked down, and I ran through my pre-flight, 'to do' list. I had to shower, gas the car, and run inside the rental car office to give my rental agent, Terrika a thank you card for her amazing customer service. I smiled, thinking about how she'd upgraded me from an economy car to a luxury, red convertible sports car.

While picturing Terrika, it intuitively hit me that my checkbook was at my hotel back in Durham. I immediately recalled Angel, the desk clerk, because she was kind. I thought about the number of patrons that might've been in my hotel room since I had checked out. This thought made me nervous. I quickly changed my nervous thoughts back to my original, 'all is well' frequency. I dialed the hotel. Guess who answered the phone?
"Hi Angel," I said, giving her my name. "I stayed there Friday and..."

She finished my sentence. "...and you left a checkbook right?"

"Yes Ma'am!" I said, glancing at Momma who was grinning more than me.

Angel said, "If I hadn't heard from you by 5:00 PM today I was going to mail it to you."

I thanked her and said, "I'll swing by and grab it on the way to the airport."

"Well, I'll see you in a little bit."

"Yes Ma'am!" I hung up, beaming that it all had come together.

I ran my errands, got thank you cards to Angel, to the maid who found my checkbook, to Terrika, and to the manager at the car rental office, and made my plane in record time.

Projecting Energy WITH YOUR HEART

Your Heart Chakra is always projecting appreciation, gratitude, kindness and sincerity. Each of these attributes are extensions of the love you had before and during this lifetime.

Briefly describe a moment when you felt pure love pouring toward you and through you.

_____

_____

Projecting Energy WITH YOUR MIND

Remember, your mind is about your greater consciousness. Your whole self is always projecting thoughts, feelings, and frequencies into every single area of your life. It's your job to make these thoughts as pure as you can.

What can you do to have more power over your thoughts?

_____

_____

Projecting Energy WITH YOUR SOUL

The eternal consciousness we know as our soul is simultaneously projecting energy back in time, in our present reality, and far into our future realities. The great thing about our soul is that it holds us in an energetic place of wholeness.

Write down a time when you felt you were inside the light of your soul.

_____

_____

Projecting Energy WITH YOUR WHOLE BEING

Think back to a time when you felt total relaxation or peace of mind. Remember a time in your life when you were having fun, enjoying your surroundings, and feeling self assured. This is another way to be in tune with your heart, mind, and soul.

What can you do to be even more in sync with your heart, mind, and soul?

_____
_____
_____
_____
_____
_____
_____
_____
_____
_____

How To Use Sending Light

I first learned how to send light from my friend, Barbara. We met working together in retail, and before I was promoted to a new job in a neighboring city, we often talked about our psychic abilities and metaphysics.

One day, Barbara was running an errand and had an impulse to stop by and see me at my new store. Her timing was perfect because I was seriously thinking of quitting my job right then. Sensing my stress, Barbara suggested I send waves of white light to upper management, the store, my office space, the employees, and everything around me.

"How do I send light?" I asked.

Barbara explained two methods. One approach is to simply visualize light surrounding the object you're focused on. You can visualize sending light with your eyes open or closed. I do both. Whether you're meditating, hiking, or sitting on an airplane you can send light.

The second way to send this healing energy is to visualize yourself bringing the light down from the Universe. As the light enters your Crown Chakra and penetrates your Heart Chakra, you can send the light out to your surroundings.

The first time I sent light I thought it was woo woo. But I was desperate, and I'm thrilled to say that sending light works. Things got easier at the new job, I got clear about how I wanted to feel in my new position, and what I wanted to experience daily. All while sending light.

I soon attracted an amazing managerial position in a new store, making more money, creating my own schedule, and beginning my writing career with the extra time I now had. Sending light is especially good when you feel you can't be objective about a situation. If the situation you're dealing with gets too personal for you, take a step back and send light. Do this simple thing, and everything will improve.

Sending Light FROM THE HEART

I love the movie "Somewhere in Time." Immediately I admired its picturesque scenery, peaceful soundtrack, and timeless message about love. While sitting in the theater over three decades ago, I knew one day I would visit the Grand Hotel on Mackinac Island where the movie was made, and reconnect with the splendor of this film and its significance to me.

From the moment I experienced the film, I instinctively sent light so I might actually have the privilege of visiting the Grand Hotel. My soul was so connected to the film's message that I inherently knew my heart's desire would someday bring me to Mackinac Island.

Years passed, life swept forward, and my spiritual work flowed, which is how I met, Mike and Ramona who'd joined me for my 2001 Peru Tour. While in Peru everyone in our group commented on wanting a relationship like theirs.

Imagine how honored I was when Mike and Ramona asked me facilitate a recommitment ceremony to commemorate their 25th anniversary, along with their gorgeous family, on Mackinac Island… in the actual, "Somewhere in Time" gazebo … at the Grand Hotel… where the movie was filmed!

I could hardly believe my ears when they asked me to be a part of their magnificent day.

I'd never forgotten the movie or my desire to visit the location where it was filmed. Each time the film crossed my mind, my soul would light up. I held this connection in my heart for decades, and over time it was this energy that brought my physical body to the exact place my heart, mind, and soul had fantasized.

Another divine component of Mike and Ramona's recommitment service was that they invited our Peru friends! Ellen, Jane, Patrick, Yvonne, and James, also attended their three-day Grand Hotel experience of love and spiritual reconnection.

Wherever we send pure light, its manifestation is out there waiting for us, Somewhere in Time.

Sending Light WITH YOUR HEART

Your Heart Chakra is the energy center where happiness, joy and compassion live, breathe, and emanate. It's been said the Heart Chakra is not of the heavens nor the earth, but is the chakra that marries our heaven and earth selves together as one.

Relax, allow the healing energy of light into your heart. What did you experience?

_____

_____

Sending Light WITH YOUR MIND

Metaphysicians say, there is only one Universal Mind, and this oneness is the order of the universe. Our mind is the builder of our realities, especially when we deliberately use our higher mind in harmony with our feelings to build our physical realities.

Breathe the healing energy of light into your mind. What did you experience?

_____

_____

Sending Light WITH YOUR SOUL

The soul is immortal. It continues to live and breathe long after our bodies expire. The light of the universe and the light that lives inside of our soul are one and the same energy. Light is consciousness. Light is love. Your soul light loves you and guides you.

Pull the healing energy of light into your soul. What was your experience?

_____

_____

Sending Light WITH YOUR WHOLE BEING

Remember back to a time you wanted something big, that felt way outside of your belief system. Think how badly you wanted it. Now recall how amazing you felt when you got it. That feeling you experienced was your heart, mind, and soul trinity activated as one.

Breathe the healing energy of light into your whole being. What are your experiences?

_____
_____
_____
_____
_____
_____
_____
_____
_____
_____
_____

How To Use Think It, INK IT

Think It, INK IT is one of my favorite hi-frequency workshops to teach because most people's minds are like walking headfirst into a whirlwind, getting spun around and spit back out in an entirely different direction. Humans are amazing at multitasking, *but* spreading ourselves too thin through multitasking doesn't work for us.

Illuminated Thought, or IT, is an actionable way to purely focus our minds on a particular subject or plan, thereby generating more enlightenment. Or what I call, en-BRIGHT-enment!

IT is a lovely remedy to harness our scattered thoughts. Writing, in and of itself, calls for streamlined focus and detailed concentration. Writing doesn't slow our brain down, it forces our brain to be in the moment. Anytime we think thoughts that light us up, we illuminate. Inking these illuminated thoughts on paper focuses our hi-frequency desires with fewer contradictions from our low-frequency habits, patterns and beliefs.

Think IT, INK IT is a fluid tool to express to the Universe how you most desire the next leg of your trip to look, feel, and be! Remember, you're mostly nonphysical energy living in a little meat-suit, and you now have a lot more tools to help you summon your soul's pure, positive energy.

Get relaxed. Allow fluid thoughts and feelings to move through you and allow your inner guidance system to merge with your heart, mind, and soul.

Think It, INK IT FROM THE HEART

I've always enjoyed writing notes. For me, writing is a soulful way to stay firmly rooted in my soul's light. Most people choose negativity over feeling good, but I've learned to relax before my negativity gets the best of me. Like the night I was on a 747 for three hours, sitting on the tarmac in Burbank, California.

The air conditioner died in the first hour, as the crew handed out bottled water to belligerent passengers. While people went berserk, I listened to music in my head phones, wrote my favorite travel affirmations, and drew pictures, grounding me deeper in the luxurious feelings that my trip would be successful.

The contrast between my feeling good, while passengers around me acted hateful, was palpable. When a wave of negativity rolled through me I asked, "Is there anything I can do to put this plane in the air?" I answered, "No," took a breath, and turned up the music.

We landed in Vegas to pandemonium. The passengers were like wild animals pushing people out of their way. I got to my departure gate to find the airline had moved our original gate clear across the airport! I gave my ticket to the associate who asked me to move to his side, just as another herd of barking passengers descended upon us. I waited as he spoke over the mob about which gate to go to and in a flash, they were gone. I grabbed my luggage to follow them, but the associate stopped me while typing away on his computer. I forgot he had my ticket.

"I've been in customer service a long time and I can spot a good customer," he said handing me a new ticket. I shook his hand and thanked him a dozen times.

"You'll find this seat more comfortable." Happy for his help, I thanked him again and flew like the wind to make my plane. After boarding, I looked for my seat number. I'd been upgraded to First Class!

Think It, INK IT WITH YOUR HEART

The Heart Chakra is about loving and being loved. It's the way we form relationships with people, animals, and the world around us. The most important love affair we should cultivate first, is the one we have with ourselves.

From your heart's perspective, write five things you spend time focusing on.

_____

_____

Think It, INK IT WITH YOUR MIND

The Universal Mind is expanded consciousness. You are not here to focus on the same thing, day in and day out. You are here to think outside the box. Writing your desires regularly, is a simple way to feel seen and heard by the universe.

From your mind's perspective, write five things you spend time focusing on.

_____

_____

Think It, INK IT WITH YOUR SOUL

Our soul is the energetic being that animates our bodies with life purpose. Let's think of our soul as an invisible bridge of light that we mentally and spiritually cross nearly 60,000 times a day, using our thoughts, feelings, and frequencies.

From your soul's perspective, write five things you spend time focusing on.

_____

_____

Think It, INK IT WITH YOUR WHOLE BEING

Life is about being conscious. It's about being connected to our source energy because it makes us happy, and gives us a sense of our unique place on this planet and beyond. Ideally, life is supposed to be about living from our heart, mind, and soul.

From your heart, mind, and soul perspective, what do you focus on most?

_____
_____
_____
_____
_____
_____
_____
_____
_____
_____

How To Use Work IT Out

Working IT Out is a great way to gain clarity. I've been interested in metaphysics, international travel, and psychic phenomenon since childhood. I didn't consciously understand my attraction to IT, I just knew I would light up every time I experienced these things.

For me, other aspects of Illuminated Thoughts were reading, writing, teaching, coaching, speaking, studying comedians, directing, and storytelling. I was attracted to all of these topics long before they became my daily reality. For instance, I knew firsthand that a teacher passionate about their craft could positively influence another person's life. Books, movies, humorists, music, or a great speaker can give us a new perspective and open our hearts to the light we possess inside.

Today I recognized that when I "Work It Out," and focus my Illuminated Thoughts on these subjects, my dormant Illuminated Talents in these areas were activated. Pay attention to thoughts and subjects that illuminate you from the inside out. These Illuminated Thoughts are gateways to a stream of dormant soul talents you possess.

I recently realized that my personal "Work IT Out" methodology was the spiritual hand guiding every class, psychic reading, and world tour I've led. Reading and touring led me to put a light hearted spin on serious subjects in my own life, which enables me to empower others to let go of their habitual low-frequency beliefs.

What are your Illuminated Thoughts about? What are your Illuminated Talents saying to you on a soul level? What have you always been drawn to do and be?

Work It Out FROM THE HEART

Growing up back home in North Carolina we had a huge patch of woods that flanked three sides of our property and an amazing creek filled with crawdads, snapping turtles, bullfrogs, salamanders, and water moccasins. The creek was especially great on hot summer days when Momma let us play in it. My favorite thing to do was sit on the banks and study the diamonds of light that reflected off the water's surface. The vibrancy of the creek and its grounding energy seemed to light me up from the inside out.

We were poor as church mice growing up, but I had a super rich imagination, and boy oh boy it took me places. Though I was sitting in the backwoods daydreaming, my imagination always took me to all kinds of beautiful places that I'd seen on television and in books. I remember seeing TV specials about the Florida Keys, the Bahamas, Mexico, Hawaii, and a stunning film of divers swimming with dolphins and whales in the Mediterranean Sea.

Along the creek bank, with my bare feet submerged in the cool water, my thoughts were lit afire with images of other oceans, continents, nations, and people.

My thoughts and feelings were illuminated with happy images, ideas, and pictures. I'd sketch in the woods and by the creek. For me, nature was my best friend and playmate. At the time I always felt seen and supported by nature in a way that I didn't feel from people.

Looking back, it's abundantly clear that I was sending my illuminated thoughts and feelings far into the reaches of my future. Today I'm thrilled to say that I've had the privilege of traveling the world teaching metaphysical principles, and giving private lectures from China to Peru, and from Alaska to the black sand beaches of Hawaii.

Work IT Out WITH YOUR HEART

Remember, 'IT' is an acronym for Illuminated Thought. There are three stages to our Heart Chakra. They are open, closed and balanced. It's been my experience that when we consciously choose to think bright, happy thoughts our hearts open fully.

How will you deliberately choose to shine your light today?

_____

_____

Work IT Out WITH YOUR MIND

When we consciously focus our attention on expanded thoughts, our whole soul-self becomes a miracle magnet, attracting greater happiness and wellness in every single area of our lives.

What thoughts cause your mind to shine?

_____

_____

Work IT Out WITH YOUR SOUL

The best kind of love is the type that awakens our soul to new opportunities and greater desires beyond anything we've ever thought before. It's the kind of love that calls us out to play in the light of All That Is.

What are your favorite soul inspired activities?

_____

_____

Work IT Out WITH YOUR WHOLE BEING

We are part of the whole that we call Oneness. My thoughts affect you. Your thoughts affect me on a deeper level that is beyond what we are consciously able to understand. When we share our heart, mind, and soul, we are sharing all that is love. Be love now.

How can you strengthen your personal connection in your heart, mind, and soul?

_____
_____
_____
_____
_____
_____
_____
_____
_____
_____

How To Use YES-ercising

We've all done some form of exercising. I've simply added, Your Electromagnetic Soul, or Y.E.S., to my exercise regimen. The Universe is unconditional love; it only responds with an enormous YES to every thought we think, feeling we feel, and question we ask.

I call it "Your Electromagnetic Soul" because we are electromagnetic. Our bodies send electrical frequencies to the Universe and the Universe magnetically matches perfectly what we're vibrating. It's our job to harness the type of electric energy that we want to send out.

YES-ercising is repeatedly improving our heart, mind, and our inspired actions by saying, "Yes" to everything in our lives that uplifts us.

If the Universe says YES to every thought, feeling, word, and action we take, wouldn't it behoove us to stop focusing on limitations, and start saying YES to uplifting subjects?

When you wake up, begin YES-ercising. Saying YES to a good night's sleep, YES to establishing a powerful intention, and YES to your fabulous trip. If there are things bringing us down, we shouldn't choose to look at these things early in the day.

Why? Because we're setting our tone for the day. Instead of seeing, hearing, and feeling negative things for the Universe to bring us, we want to be lifted up into feel-good feelings. If we're numb and stuck in negativity, the Universe will only bring us negative things. But if we're uplifted, the Universe will bring us good things.

As you head to your next destination, be sure to exercise saying YES to beautiful surroundings, YES to all of your mystical, healing experiences, YES, to creating a fantastic frequency for yourself, and a loud YES to living in your highest and best self.

YES-ercising FROM THE HEART

When I was a kid I loved watching television. It was one of my favorite ways to be transported from the reality of my poor family's single wide trailer, and see other worlds beyond.

I would eagerly lie on the floor watching travel shows that featured marine biologist, Jacques Cousteau, and beam with joy when Marlin Perkins of Mutual of Omaha's Wild Kingdom explored different continents.

I was also a huge fan of Hawaii 5-0. Heck, just the theme song lifted my frequency through the roof as I shimmy-shimmy-coco-bopped to the drums and horns. Of course, I only did that in my mind. It was a trailer after all. In the south. In the 1960s.

From Hawaii 5-0 I learned to say, Mele Kalikimaka, which means, "Merry Christmas." I liked learning something new and loved how the words rolled off my tongue. Right then, I knew that somehow I would visit Hawaii and other parts of the world so that I could live these kinds of experiences in real time. It was an inner feeling, a deep, rich knowing that I had, and it was as real to me as the thin brown plywood walls behind our television set.

I didn't know it at the time, but I had activated a sincere series of desires through YES-ercising. I was purely thinking, feeling, and radiating powerful YES energy to traveling, seeing the world, and interacting with new people and places that were beautifully different from my simple reality.

Today I know that appreciating other parts of the world, new languages, or unfamiliar traditions causes us to vibrate at a higher energy. As a student of gratitude, I've also learned to intuitively harness these pure frequencies to enhance my life while uplifting others.

Until we meet again, Aloha, and if I don't see you during the holidays, Mele Kalikimaka!

YES-ercising WITH YOUR HEART

Our Universal Heart is the gateway to higher realms of consciousness. It's also the vehicle that moves love through every atom, cell, and molecule of our bodies. When we love ourselves, we merge our purest physical and nonphysical energies as one.

How many hi-frequency things can your heart say YES to now?

_____

_____

YES-ercising WITH YOUR MIND

We create our reality with the thoughts we think and the feelings we feel. There is only a small percentage of people who understand that this is the way we create our lives. In essence, we are either creating great prosperity or great poverty. It's our choice.

In what areas does your miraculous mind say, YES the most?

_____

_____

YES-ercising WITH YOUR SOUL

Our soul is the divine truth of that which we are. It is perfection in action. Its always dancing between the invisible and visible worlds weaving its magic, based solely on our habitual thoughts and feelings.

In one sentence, what do you want your soul to know? Why?

_____

_____

YES-ercising WITH YOUR WHOLE BEING

With every thought and feeling we entertain, we have the greatest choice of all. As conscious creators, we can deliberately focus our attention on joy and happiness in this amazing game called life – or not choose anything.

Please, finish this sentence, I can feel my heart, mind, and soul most when I…

_____
_____
_____
_____
_____
_____
_____
_____
_____
_____
_____

How To Use ZEN-tention

ZEN-tention is about achieving enlightenment through meditative contemplation. This manifests itself as a relaxed intention we feel inside our heart, mind, and soul.

It's important to be thoughtful about our intentions and to remember that everything we choose to think about should be focused on our purest thoughts, feelings, and desires.

Pay close attention to your neutral, often vanilla intentions, and then froth them up to a lighter, easier space of peace within.

A lot of us fall into the same unconscious cycle of blindly stating low-frequency intentions that just get us by. Instead of blurting out intentions while rushing through hotel lobbies, or catching my next plane, bus or train, I started establishing intentions as soon as the morning alarm went off.

Throughout the day I continued this bliss with a steady stream of meditative, Zen-like intentions. One day, while practicing this, the word "ZEN-tention" flashed across the screen in my mind's eye, and I've loved stating new ZEN-tentions ever since.

ZEN-tention FROM THE HEART

My Momma was one of the hardest working people I've ever known. Every time she put her mind to something, she was hell bent and determined to get it done and done right, and she expected the same from us kids. She didn't know how to relax or sit still; all she understood was work, even on her days off. Growing up I would've bet big money that nothing and nobody could budge Momma's strict, tough as nails work ethic – until the first day I saw her at the beach.

The beach transformed Momma into a relaxed, more thoughtful, and lighthearted person. Being at the ocean brought the light back to Momma's eyes.

Somehow the ocean's energy made her calm, which allowed us kids a long weekend to spend time with the best version of her. It was miraculous to see, considering Momma always worked so hard to lift our family out of back-breaking poverty.

Our intention as a family was to visit the beach for a day or two when we could afford it, but somewhere between this basic intention and arriving at the Atlantic Ocean, Momma's disposition miraculously switched from hard working woman to an almost Zen-like person.

I know now that I was watching Momma go from intention into a masterful Zen-tention. We all have areas in our lives where we transcend our old programming and rise up into our best selves.

The beach did that for Momma. For me it's Machu Picchu, tropical destinations, and new cultures filled with strong community all around the world.

ZEN-tention WITH YOUR HEART

What dominant feelings are in your heart? Are they mostly happy, or sad? Do they feel bad more often than good? It takes practice to train your heart-mind to move back toward its natural feeling of happily-ever-after. I promise, it's worth the practice.

What does it feel like to be completely relaxed, in your heart?

_____

_____

ZEN-tention WITH YOUR MIND

Beyond the circuitries of our body and mind; we are also able to enter into the invisible worlds that created our current reality based on our thoughts and feelings. These worlds vibrate at a such a high frequency, that we can't physically see or hear them.

When are you the absolute most relaxed in your mind?

_____

_____

ZEN-tention WITH YOUR SOUL

Its been said that humans have carbon in their souls, and that they are stardust with people names. It's true. I believe that as you're reading this, the greater part of you is shining its star light from the higher dimensions, down on you. And smiling.

How does your soul encourage you to relax?

_____

_____

ZEN-tention WITH YOUR WHOLE BEING

Isn't it lovely when we have a conscious intention and follow it through to the end? It feels nice to be living in the delicious flow of All Is Well. Especially when we enjoy creating the time and space inside our heart, mind, and soul to make our lives better.

List moments when you're most in tune with your heart, mind, and soul.

_____
_____
_____
_____
_____
_____
_____
_____
_____
_____

YOUR TRAVEL JOURNAL

Machu Picchu

The Great Wall of China

Chichen Itza

Taj Mahal

Stonehenge

Petra Jordan

Date _____ Place _____

Today's Itinerary

_____
_____
_____
_____
_____
_____
_____
_____
_____
_____
_____
_____
_____
_____

Weather Conditions

Temperature _____

- ☐ Sunny
- ☐ Partly Sunny
- ☐ Cloudy
- ☐ Windy
- ☐ Scattered Showers
- ☐ Rain
- ☐ Thunderstorms
- ☐ Snow/Snowy

How Are You Feeling Right Now?

Feeling Dark and Depressed — **Vanilla** — **Amazingly Happy, Joyful**

My Intention for today is...

_____
_____
_____
_____
_____
_____
_____
_____
_____

The Hi-Frequency Travel Tip(s) I Am Using Today...

☐	**Appreci-Asking**	(page 17)	☐	**Sending Light**	(page 37)
☐	**Ask Better Questions**	(page 21)	☐	**Think IT, INK IT**	(page 41)
☐	**Mirror Soul Speak**	(page 25)	☐	**Work IT Out**	(page 45)
☐	**Power Word Lullabies**	(page 29)	☐	**YES-cercising**	(page 49)
☐	**Projecting Energy**	(page 33)	☐	**ZEN-tention**	(page 53)

Unforgettable Experiences I Had Today...

The Sphinx, Egypt

"Appreci-Asking is a pure way we hold unconditional love in our hearts while subconsciously asking the Universe for even more love."

Scuba Diver and Sea Turtle

Pearl River, Louisiana Bayou

"Each and every day I choose to think Illuminated Thoughts and in return I experience Illuminated Travel experiences."

Date _____   Place _____

Today's Itinerary

_____
_____
_____
_____
_____
_____
_____
_____
_____
_____
_____
_____
_____
_____

Weather Conditions

Temperature _____

- ☐ Sunny
- ☐ Partly Sunny
- ☐ Cloudy
- ☐ Windy
- ☐ Scattered Showers
- ☐ Rain
- ☐ Thunderstorms
- ☐ Snow/Snowy

How Are You Feeling Right Now?

Feeling Dark and Depressed — **Vanilla** — **Amazingly Happy, Joyful**

My Intention for today is...

_____
_____
_____
_____
_____
_____
_____
_____

The Hi-Frequency Travel Tip(s) I Am Using Today...

☐	**Appreci-Asking**	(page 17)	☐	**Sending Light**	(page 37)
☐	**Ask Better Questions**	(page 21)	☐	**Think IT, INK IT**	(page 41)
☐	**Mirror Soul Speak**	(page 25)	☐	**Work IT Out**	(page 45)
☐	**Power Word Lullabies**	(page 29)	☐	**YES-cercising**	(page 49)
☐	**Projecting Energy**	(page 33)	☐	**ZEN-tention**	(page 53)

Unforgettable Experiences I Had Today…

Sweetheart Abbey, Scotland

"I focus my undivided attention on my heart's desire. These focused feelings easily put me in perfect alignment with the Universe's unconditional love."

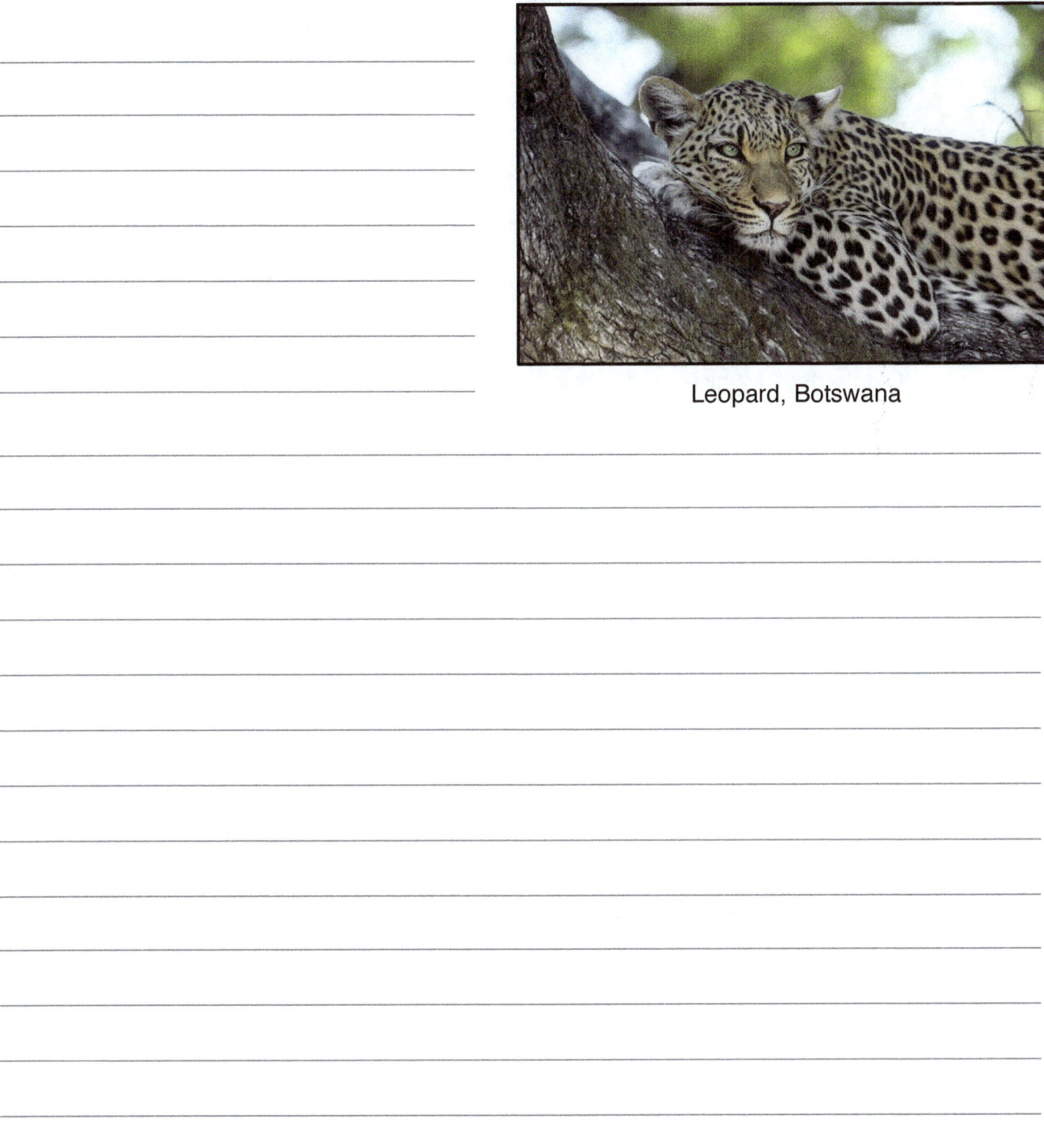

Leopard, Botswana

Oktoberfest, Munich

"I love acknowledging the power of frequency because it's an invisible energy that can lift our consciousness higher into prosperity, or slam us down into the darkest bowels of poverty. It's always our choice."

Date _____ Place _____

Today's Itinerary

_____
_____
_____
_____
_____
_____
_____
_____
_____
_____
_____
_____
_____
_____

Weather Conditions

Temperature _____

- ☐ Sunny
- ☐ Partly Sunny
- ☐ Cloudy
- ☐ Windy
- ☐ Scattered Showers
- ☐ Rain
- ☐ Thunderstorms
- ☐ Snow/Snowy

How Are You Feeling Right Now?

Feeling Dark and Depressed — **Vanilla** — **Amazingly Happy, Joyful**

My Intention for today is...

_____
_____
_____
_____
_____
_____
_____
_____

The Hi-Frequency Travel Tip(s) I Am Using Today...

☐	**Appreci-Asking**	(page 17)	☐ **Sending Light**	(page 37)
☐	**Ask Better Questions**	(page 21)	☐ **Think IT, INK IT**	(page 41)
☐	**Mirror Soul Speak**	(page 25)	☐ **Work IT Out**	(page 45)
☐	**Power Word Lullabies**	(page 29)	☐ **YES-cercising**	(page 49)
☐	**Projecting Energy**	(page 33)	☐ **ZEN-tention**	(page 53)

Unforgettable Experiences I Had Today...

Banteay Srei Temple, Cambodia

"I love basking in happy, joyful thoughts because these same thought frequencies will manifest themselves as happy, joyful people, places, circumstances, and situations in my future."

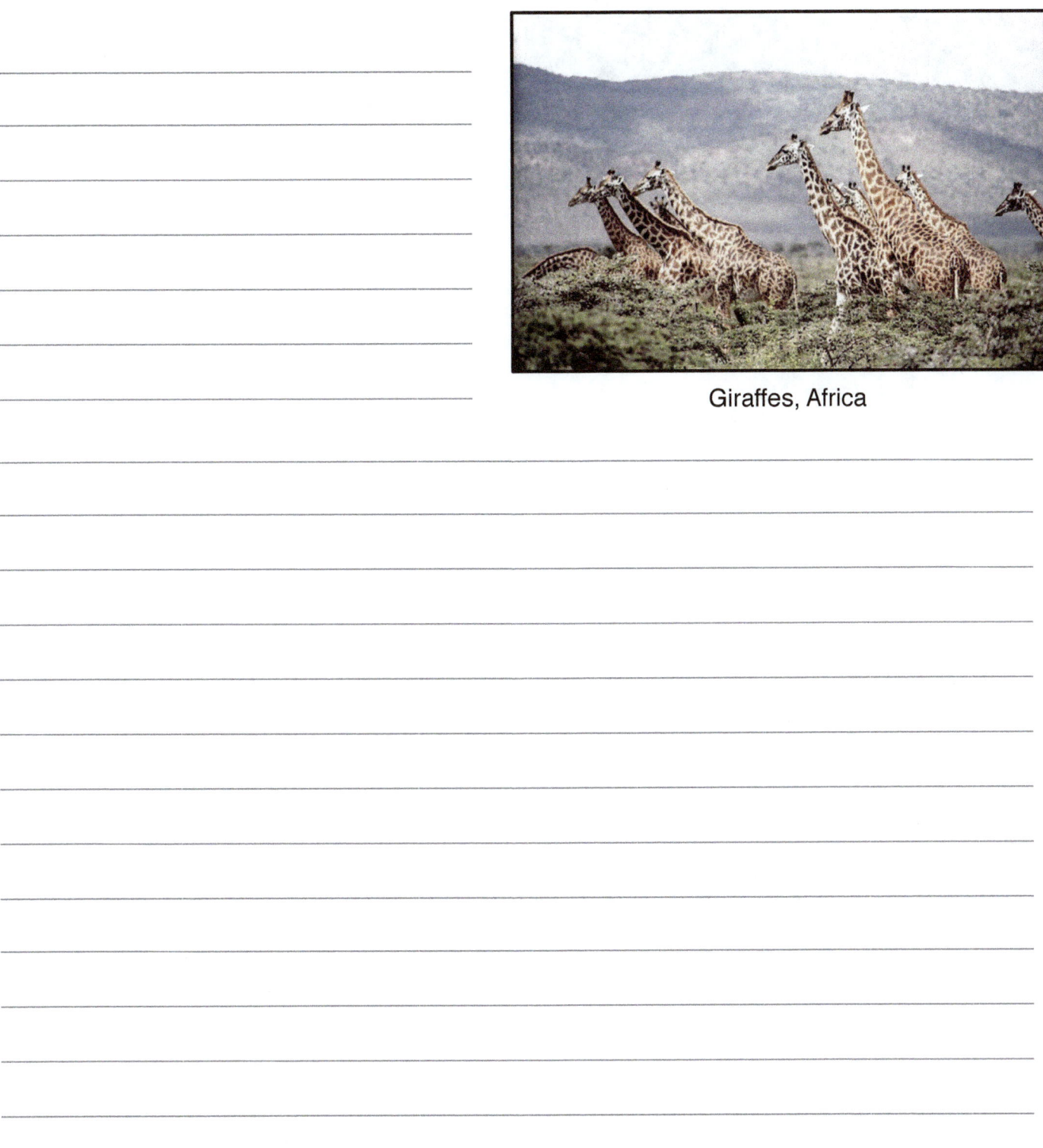
Giraffes, Africa

Las Vegas, Nevada

"ZEN-tention: Achieving enlightenment through meditative contemplation while holding pure intentions in your mind, your heart, and spirit. This peaceful state of being often leads to blissful moments, relaxation, and greater peace!"

Date _____   Place _____

Today's Itinerary

_____
_____
_____
_____
_____
_____
_____
_____
_____
_____
_____
_____
_____

Weather Conditions

Temperature _____
- ☐ Sunny
- ☐ Partly Sunny
- ☐ Cloudy
- ☐ Windy
- ☐ Scattered Showers
- ☐ Rain
- ☐ Thunderstorms
- ☐ Snow/Snowy

How Are You Feeling Right Now?

Feeling Dark and Depressed — **Vanilla** — **Amazingly Happy, Joyful**

My Intention for today is...

_____
_____
_____
_____
_____
_____
_____
_____

The Hi-Frequency Travel Tip(s) I Am Using Today…

☐	**Appreci-Asking**	(page 17)	☐ **Sending Light**	(page 37)
☐	**Ask Better Questions**	(page 21)	☐ **Think IT, INK IT**	(page 41)
☐	**Mirror Soul Speak**	(page 25)	☐ **Work IT Out**	(page 45)
☐	**Power Word Lullabies**	(page 29)	☐ **YES-cercising**	(page 49)
☐	**Projecting Energy**	(page 33)	☐ **ZEN-tention**	(page 53)

Unforgettable Experiences I Had Today…

St. Basil's, Moscow

"As a Soul Intuitive, I've worked with the spiritual realm my whole life. Whether you know it or not, you have always been supported by the Universe, nonphysical beings, energetic influences, and of course, by your own soul!"

Ostriches, Africa

Ireland Coast

"Every day when I appreciate the beauty, grace, and happiness around me, the Universe brings me more."

Date _____   Place _____

Today's Itinerary

_____
_____
_____
_____
_____
_____
_____
_____
_____
_____
_____
_____
_____
_____

Weather Conditions

Temperature _____

- ☐ Sunny
- ☐ Partly Sunny
- ☐ Cloudy
- ☐ Windy
- ☐ Scattered Showers
- ☐ Rain
- ☐ Thunderstorms
- ☐ Snow/Snowy

How Are You Feeling Right Now?

Feeling Dark and Depressed — **Vanilla** — **Amazingly Happy, Joyful**

My Intention for today is...

_____
_____
_____
_____
_____
_____
_____
_____

The Hi-Frequency Travel Tip(s) I Am Using Today…

☐	**Appreci-Asking**	(page 17)	☐ **Sending Light**	(page 37)
☐	**Ask Better Questions**	(page 21)	☐ **Think IT, INK IT**	(page 41)
☐	**Mirror Soul Speak**	(page 25)	☐ **Work IT Out**	(page 45)
☐	**Power Word Lullabies**	(page 29)	☐ **YES-cercising**	(page 49)
☐	**Projecting Energy**	(page 33)	☐ **ZEN-tention**	(page 53)

Unforgettable Experiences I Had Today…

Big Ben, London

"My heart says yes to travel, yes to meeting new people, and yes to sharing my authentic self with others on my spiritual path."

Elephants, Africa

Corona Arch, Utah

"If you're like me, you're shy about standing in front of a mirror – especially naked. Please don't be. Practicing Mirror Soul Speak is a soft, powerful way to deliberately elevate your old thoughts into prosperity consciousness."

Date _____   Place _____

Today's Itinerary

_____
_____
_____
_____
_____
_____
_____
_____
_____
_____
_____
_____
_____
_____
_____
_____
_____

Weather Conditions

Temperature _____

- ☐ Sunny
- ☐ Partly Sunny
- ☐ Cloudy
- ☐ Windy
- ☐ Scattered Showers
- ☐ Rain
- ☐ Thunderstorms
- ☐ Snow/Snowy

How Are You Feeling Right Now?

Feeling Dark and Depressed — **Vanilla** — **Amazingly Happy, Joyful**

My Intention for today is...

_____
_____
_____
_____
_____
_____
_____
_____

The Hi-Frequency Travel Tip(s) I Am Using Today...

☐	**Appreci-Asking**	(page 17)	☐ **Sending Light**	(page 37)
☐	**Ask Better Questions**	(page 21)	☐ **Think IT, INK IT**	(page 41)
☐	**Mirror Soul Speak**	(page 25)	☐ **Work IT Out**	(page 45)
☐	**Power Word Lullabies**	(page 29)	☐ **YES-cercising**	(page 49)
☐	**Projecting Energy**	(page 33)	☐ **ZEN-tention**	(page 53)

Unforgettable Experiences I Had Today…

Maui, Hawaii

"Pay attention to thoughts and subjects that light you up. Illuminated Thoughts are gateways to streams of existing soul gifts you possess within."

Mardi Gras, New Orleans

Wat Pho Temple, Bangkok

"I quietly sit in peaceful moments, and I allow these peaceful moments to fill me up from the top of my head to the tips of my toes."

Date _____   Place _____

Today's Itinerary

_____
_____
_____
_____
_____
_____
_____
_____
_____
_____
_____
_____
_____

Weather Conditions

Temperature _____
- ☐ Sunny
- ☐ Partly Sunny
- ☐ Cloudy
- ☐ Windy
- ☐ Scattered Showers
- ☐ Rain
- ☐ Thunderstorms
- ☐ Snow/Snowy

How Are You Feeling Right Now?

Feeling Dark and Depressed — **Vanilla** — **Amazingly Happy, Joyful**

My Intention for today is...

_____
_____
_____
_____
_____
_____
_____
_____
_____

The Hi-Frequency Travel Tip(s) I Am Using Today...

☐	**Appreci-Asking**	(page 17)	☐	**Sending Light**	(page 37)
☐	**Ask Better Questions**	(page 21)	☐	**Think IT, INK IT**	(page 41)
☐	**Mirror Soul Speak**	(page 25)	☐	**Work IT Out**	(page 45)
☐	**Power Word Lullabies**	(page 29)	☐	**YES-cercising**	(page 49)
☐	**Projecting Energy**	(page 33)	☐	**ZEN-tention**	(page 53)

Unforgettable Experiences I Had Today...

Painted Desert, Arizona

"Think it, INK IT is a lovely remedy to harness our scattered thoughts. Anytime we think thoughts that light us up, we illuminate from the inside out. Inking these thoughts on paper causes us to focus our desires more purely."

Hot Air Balloon Races, New Mexico

98

Kuang Si Falls, Laos

 "I AM always and forever in alignment with seeing and hearing what my soul is intuitively saying."

Date _____   Place _____

Today's Itinerary

_____
_____
_____
_____
_____
_____
_____
_____
_____
_____
_____
_____
_____
_____
_____

Weather Conditions

Temperature _____
- ☐ Sunny
- ☐ Partly Sunny
- ☐ Cloudy
- ☐ Windy
- ☐ Scattered Showers
- ☐ Rain
- ☐ Thunderstorms
- ☐ Snow/Snowy

How Are You Feeling Right Now?

Feeling Dark and Depressed — **Vanilla** — **Amazingly Happy, Joyful**

My Intention for today is...

_____
_____
_____
_____
_____
_____
_____
_____
_____

The Hi-Frequency Travel Tip(s) I Am Using Today...

☐	**Appreci-Asking**	(page 17)	☐	**Sending Light**	(page 37)
☐	**Ask Better Questions**	(page 21)	☐	**Think IT, INK IT**	(page 41)
☐	**Mirror Soul Speak**	(page 25)	☐	**Work IT Out**	(page 45)
☐	**Power Word Lullabies**	(page 29)	☐	**YES-cercising**	(page 49)
☐	**Projecting Energy**	(page 33)	☐	**ZEN-tention**	(page 53)

Unforgettable Experiences I Had Today...

Golden Gate Bridge, San Francisco

"I AM the master of asking powerful questions that stir my heart, mind, and soul into greater happiness."

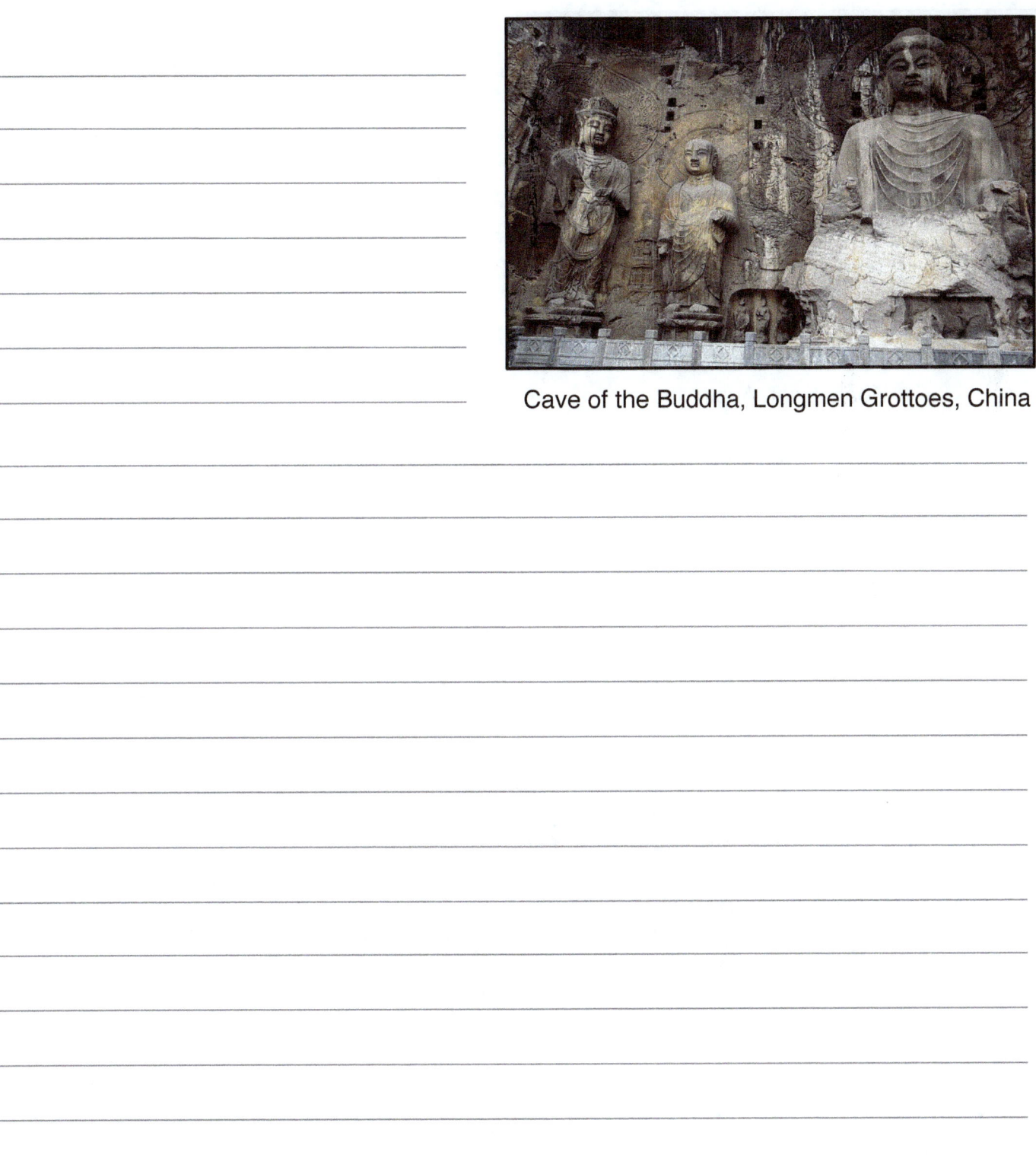
Cave of the Buddha, Longmen Grottoes, China

Koala Bear, Australia

"The first time I heard about sending light I thought it was woo woo. The good news is, I was desperate enough to try it and guess what? Sending light is an extension of our soul's core essence – and it works!"

Date _____   Place _____

Today's Itinerary

_____
_____
_____
_____
_____
_____
_____
_____
_____
_____
_____
_____
_____

Weather Conditions

Temperature _____

- ☐ Sunny
- ☐ Partly Sunny
- ☐ Cloudy
- ☐ Windy
- ☐ Scattered Showers
- ☐ Rain
- ☐ Thunderstorms
- ☐ Snow/Snowy

How Are You Feeling Right Now?

Feeling Dark and Depressed — **Vanilla** — **Amazingly Happy, Joyful**

My Intention for today is...

_____
_____
_____
_____
_____
_____
_____

The Hi-Frequency Travel Tip(s) I Am Using Today...

☐	**Appreci-Asking**	(page 17)	☐ **Sending Light**	(page 37)
☐	**Ask Better Questions**	(page 21)	☐ **Think IT, INK IT**	(page 41)
☐	**Mirror Soul Speak**	(page 25)	☐ **Work IT Out**	(page 45)
☐	**Power Word Lullabies**	(page 29)	☐ **YES-cercising**	(page 49)
☐	**Projecting Energy**	(page 33)	☐ **ZEN-tention**	(page 53)

Unforgettable Experiences I Had Today...

Grand Canyon, Arizona

"Being curious enough to ask great questions actually stimulates our brain, heart, and soul."

Camping

Dolphin

111

"Each and every day my thoughts, feelings, and frequencies are electromagnetically pulling more joy, love, and happiness to me and into all areas of my life."

Date _____   Place _____

Today's Itinerary

_____
_____
_____
_____
_____
_____
_____
_____
_____
_____
_____
_____
_____
_____
_____

Weather Conditions

Temperature _____

- ☐ Sunny
- ☐ Partly Sunny
- ☐ Cloudy
- ☐ Windy
- ☐ Scattered Showers
- ☐ Rain
- ☐ Thunderstorms
- ☐ Snow/Snowy

How Are You Feeling Right Now?

Feeling Dark and Depressed — **Vanilla** — **Amazingly Happy, Joyful**

My Intention for today is...

_____
_____
_____
_____
_____
_____
_____
_____

The Hi-Frequency Travel Tip(s) I Am Using Today...

☐	**Appreci-Asking**	(page 17)	☐ **Sending Light**	(page 37)
☐	**Ask Better Questions**	(page 21)	☐ **Think IT, INK IT**	(page 41)
☐	**Mirror Soul Speak**	(page 25)	☐ **Work IT Out**	(page 45)
☐	**Power Word Lullabies**	(page 29)	☐ **YES-cercising**	(page 49)
☐	**Projecting Energy**	(page 33)	☐ **ZEN-tention**	(page 53)

Unforgettable Experiences I Had Today...

Costa Rica

"The next time you complain about an aspect of traveling, ask yourself, 'Do I want these negative thoughts I'm having to meet me again, and again, and again during my trip?'"

Banyon Tree, Honolulu

Singapore Chinatown

"I AM light. I AM love. I AM happily sending this light and love forward into all areas of my body, mind, spirit, and life travels."

Date _____   Place _____

Today's Itinerary

_____
_____
_____
_____
_____
_____
_____
_____
_____
_____
_____
_____
_____
_____

Weather Conditions

Temperature _____
- ☐ Sunny
- ☐ Partly Sunny
- ☐ Cloudy
- ☐ Windy
- ☐ Scattered Showers
- ☐ Rain
- ☐ Thunderstorms
- ☐ Snow/Snowy

How Are You Feeling Right Now?

| Feeling Dark and Depressed | | | | Vanilla | | | | Amazingly Happy, Joyful |

My Intention for today is...

_____
_____
_____
_____
_____
_____
_____
_____

The Hi-Frequency Travel Tip(s) I Am Using Today…

☐ **Appreci-Asking**	(page 17)	☐ **Sending Light**	(page 37)
☐ **Ask Better Questions**	(page 21)	☐ **Think IT, INK IT**	(page 41)
☐ **Mirror Soul Speak**	(page 25)	☐ **Work IT Out**	(page 45)
☐ **Power Word Lullabies**	(page 29)	☐ **YES-cercising**	(page 49)
☐ **Projecting Energy**	(page 33)	☐ **ZEN-tention**	(page 53)

Unforgettable Experiences I Had Today…

Apse St. Peter Basicilca, The Vatican

"I likened lullabies to hypnotherapy techniques used to take clients deeper into a relaxed space so they may achieve their desired goals. As we speak in a lulling voice to ourselves, our conscious mind drifts deeper into a restful place."

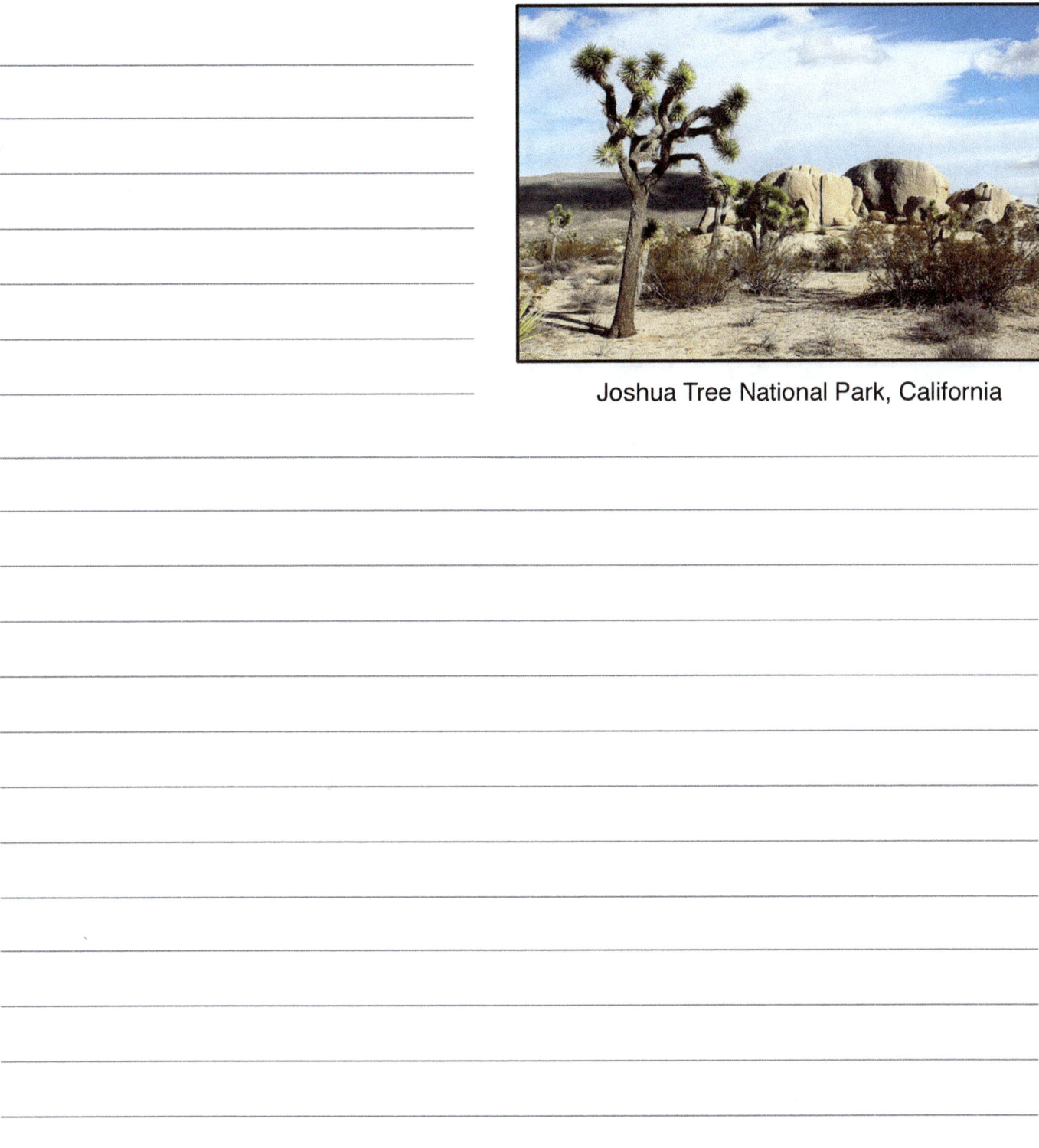
Joshua Tree National Park, California

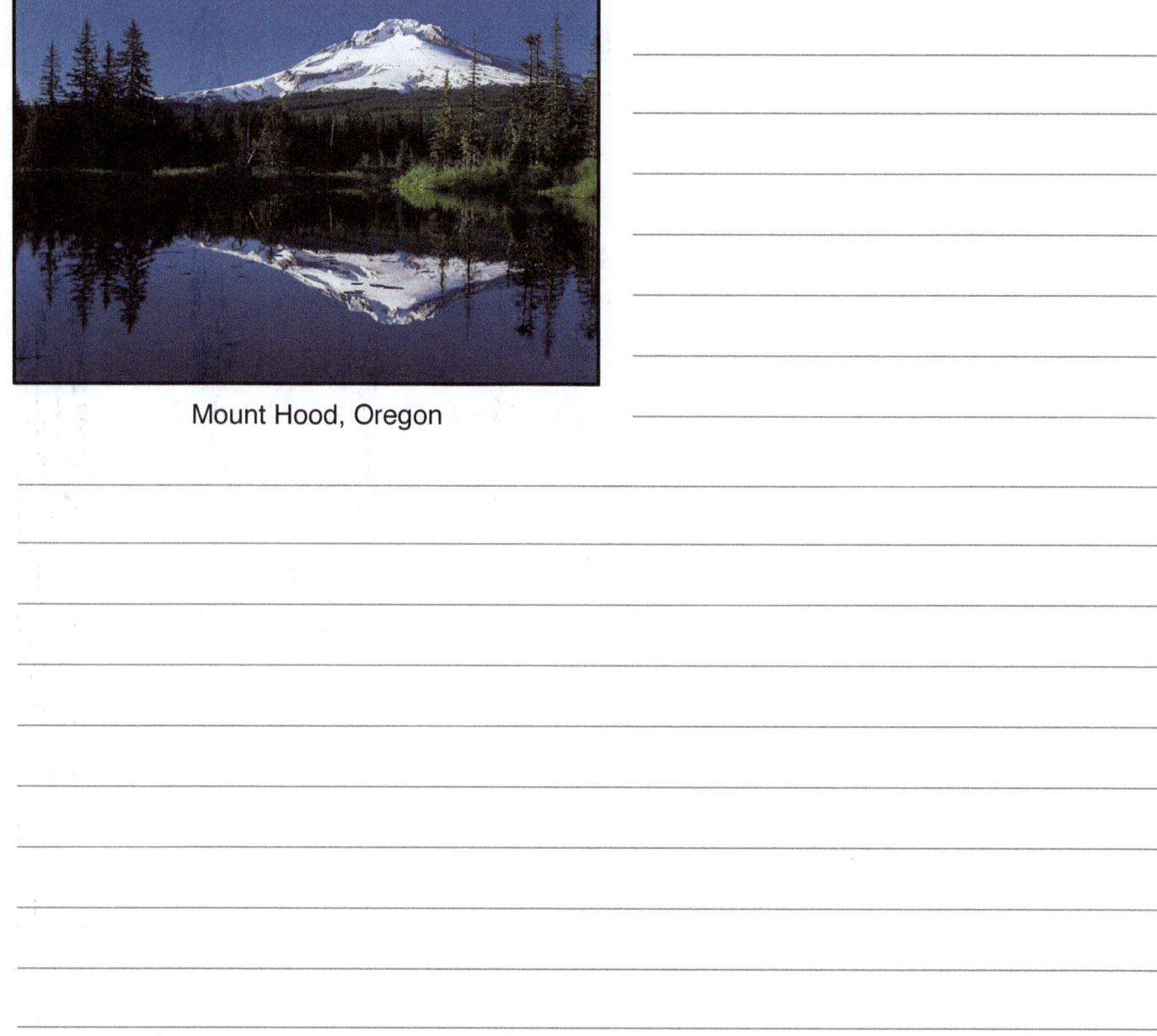
Mount Hood, Oregon

 "Every thought I think comes from my higher self. Every feeling I feel comes from my highest desire. Every pure thought and feeling I emanate produces rich results."

Date _____   Place _____

Today's Itinerary

_____
_____
_____
_____
_____
_____
_____
_____
_____
_____
_____
_____
_____
_____
_____

Weather Conditions

Temperature _____

- ☐ Sunny
- ☐ Partly Sunny
- ☐ Cloudy
- ☐ Windy
- ☐ Scattered Showers
- ☐ Rain
- ☐ Thunderstorms
- ☐ Snow/Snowy

How Are You Feeling Right Now?

Feeling Dark and Depressed — **Vanilla** — **Amazingly Happy, Joyful**

My Intention for today is...

_____
_____
_____
_____
_____
_____
_____
_____

The Hi-Frequency Travel Tip(s) I Am Using Today...

☐	**Appreci-Asking**	(page 17)	☐	**Sending Light**	(page 37)
☐	**Ask Better Questions**	(page 21)	☐	**Think IT, INK IT**	(page 41)
☐	**Mirror Soul Speak**	(page 25)	☐	**Work IT Out**	(page 45)
☐	**Power Word Lullabies**	(page 29)	☐	**YES-cercising**	(page 49)
☐	**Projecting Energy**	(page 33)	☐	**ZEN-tention**	(page 53)

Unforgettable Experiences I Had Today…

The Colosseum, Rome

"For every blade of grass, building, or ocean we see with our physical eyes, there are trillions of unseen forces that govern them, including gravity, the spirits in nature, and the law of attraction, to name a few."

US Capitol, Washington D.C.

Quan Yin, China

"In a relaxed and loving way, I quietly soothe my body and mind to sleep so my spirit and soul play and dance in the stars."

Date _____ Place _____

Today's Itinerary

_____
_____
_____
_____
_____
_____
_____
_____
_____
_____
_____
_____
_____
_____

Weather Conditions

Temperature _____

- ☐ Sunny
- ☐ Partly Sunny
- ☐ Cloudy
- ☐ Windy
- ☐ Scattered Showers
- ☐ Rain
- ☐ Thunderstorms
- ☐ Snow/Snowy

How Are You Feeling Right Now?

Feeling Dark and Depressed — **Vanilla** — **Amazingly Happy, Joyful**

My Intention for today is...

_____
_____
_____
_____
_____
_____
_____
_____

The Hi-Frequency Travel Tip(s) I Am Using Today...

☐	**Appreci-Asking**	(page 17)	☐	**Sending Light**	(page 37)
☐	**Ask Better Questions**	(page 21)	☐	**Think IT, INK IT**	(page 41)
☐	**Mirror Soul Speak**	(page 25)	☐	**Work IT Out**	(page 45)
☐	**Power Word Lullabies**	(page 29)	☐	**YES-cercising**	(page 49)
☐	**Projecting Energy**	(page 33)	☐	**ZEN-tention**	(page 53)

Unforgettable Experiences I Had Today...

Dubai Skyline

"If the Universe only says YES to every thought, feeling, word, and action we've ever had, wouldn't it behoove us to stop speaking about lack and limitation, and start saying YES to abundance?"

Times Square, New York

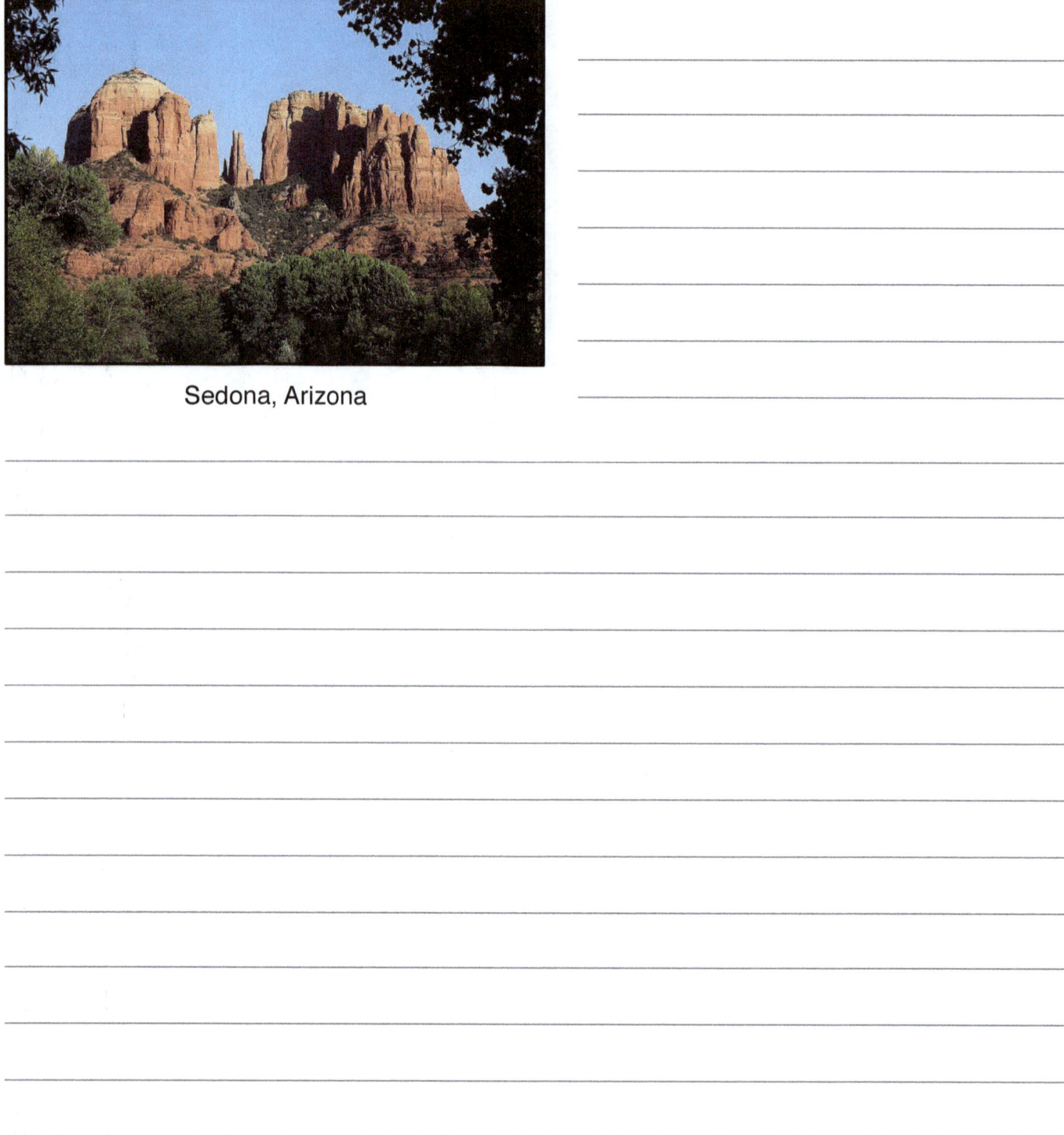

Sedona, Arizona

"I AM great at giving illuminated energy out to the world. I AM even greater at receiving illuminated healing energy from the Universe."

Date _____   Place _____

Today's Itinerary

_____
_____
_____
_____
_____
_____
_____
_____
_____
_____
_____
_____
_____
_____
_____
_____

Weather Conditions

Temperature _____

- ☐ Sunny
- ☐ Partly Sunny
- ☐ Cloudy
- ☐ Windy
- ☐ Scattered Showers
- ☐ Rain
- ☐ Thunderstorms
- ☐ Snow/Snowy

How Are You Feeling Right Now?

Feeling Dark and Depressed — **Vanilla** — **Amazingly Happy, Joyful**

My Intention for today is...

_____
_____
_____
_____
_____
_____
_____
_____

The Hi-Frequency Travel Tip(s) I Am Using Today...

☐	**Appreci-Asking**	(page 17)	☐ **Sending Light**	(page 37)
☐	**Ask Better Questions**	(page 21)	☐ **Think IT, INK IT**	(page 41)
☐	**Mirror Soul Speak**	(page 25)	☐ **Work IT Out**	(page 45)
☐	**Power Word Lullabies**	(page 29)	☐ **YES-cercising**	(page 49)
☐	**Projecting Energy**	(page 33)	☐ **ZEN-tention**	(page 53)

Unforgettable Experiences I Had Today...

Mount Rushmore, South Dakota

"It is absolutely the nonphysical world that governs our physicality. The spiritual world is more influential in creating our lives than most people know!"

Hollywood, California

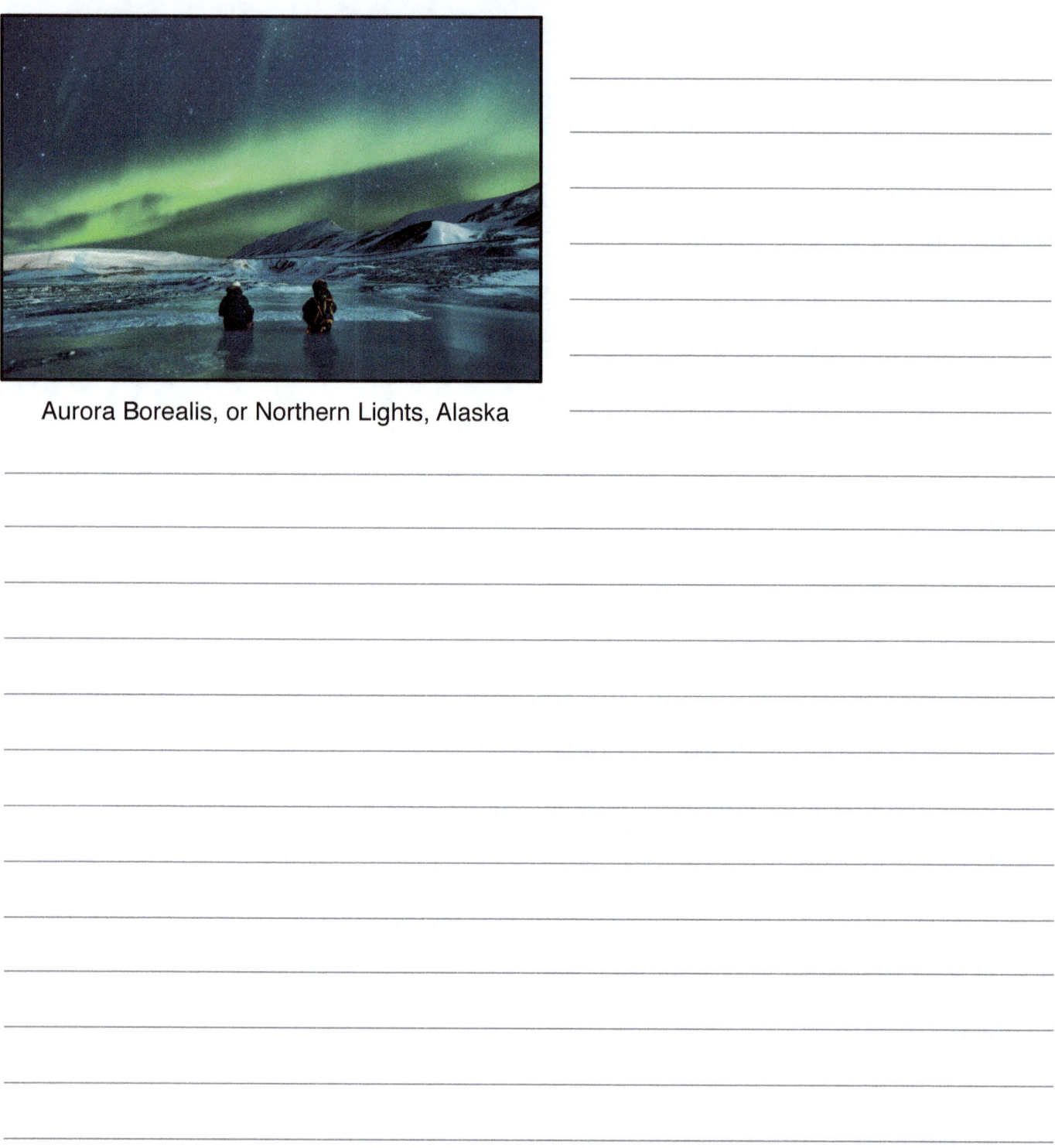
Aurora Borealis, or Northern Lights, Alaska

 "I AM brilliantly guided, divinely protected, and in perfect harmony with my higher self."

WELCOME HOME MY FRIEND

Machu Picchu

The Great Wall of China

Chichen Itza

Taj Mahal

Stonehenge

Petra Jordan

WELCOME HOME

My favorite question is, 'What arrives to my destination first, my body, or my thoughts and feelings about my destination?' The answer: it's your thoughts and feelings.

Just as you focused conscious energy getting ready for your trip, and during your trip, you also want to send pleasant thoughts and feelings upon your return home.

Spend a few moments appreciating your home. This is your private space. It mirrors your energy. The more we love our home the more our home loves us back. I get to see this first hand when returning from my travels.

I personally fill my house with light before I leave it and I do the same when I arrive. I walk into each room and allow my appreciation to bathe the walls, ceilings, and floors. I do this for a few moments, as gratitude flows through me and out to every area of my house.

I repeat this same inner exercise with my family, friends, automobile, neighborhood, and work space. I do this to keep the feel-good momentum flowing.

Sometimes I say out loud, "I love my home. I love my friends. I love the light that shines into every area of my life!" This is not a left brain exercise or a flat emotional practice, it involves as much gratitude that my heart, mind, and soul can muster. And it feels good.

Because I love these areas of my life, they love me back. The energy I put into them matches the love, safety, wellness, and protection they give in return.

For me, it's love and gratitude that meets me when I get home from traveling. Abraham-Hicks says, "Our vibration is where we last left it." My vibration about my returning home from a trip is high, fast and pure. The minute I step onto my property, the light bathes my mind and senses, greeting me much like a new puppy excited to see me when I get home from work.

Nice, right? You can have this same type of experience just by using these Hi-Frequency Travel Tips in all areas of your life. Welcome home.

TOUCHING BASE WITH YOUR FEELINGS

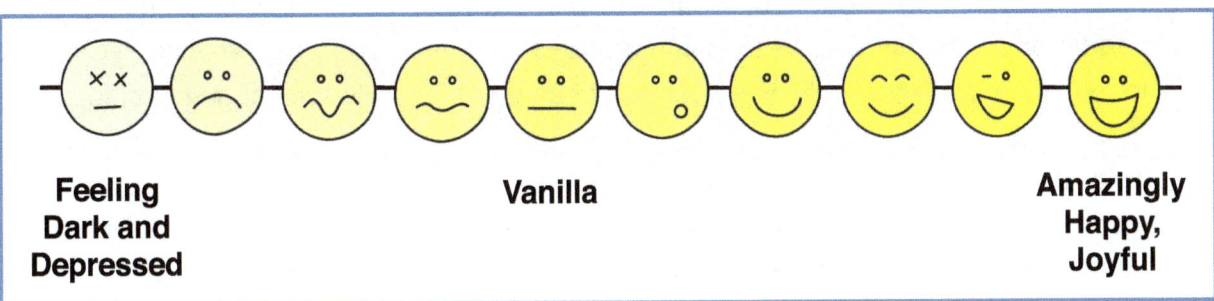

Now that you're home, how do you feel?

CHECK ONE: I feel Good _____   I feel Bad _____   I feel Vanilla _____

If you said, I feel good, how good on a scale from 1 to 10, with 10 being the best?
_____
_____
_____

Why do you feel so good? What provoked it? Be as specific as you can.
_____
_____
_____

If you said, I feel bad, how bad on a scale from 1 to 10, with 1 being the worst?
_____
_____
_____

Why do you feel bad? What provoked it? Be as specific as you can.
_____
_____
_____

RECAPPING YOUR HEART

Welcome home. Now that you're back from your lovely vacation, let's gently recap things you learned about your Heart Chakra. We possess the loving attributes of our hearts for all eternity. Our heart communicates with us through our feelings. It's our job to pay attention to our feelings so our heart can guide us in its true language of love.

Take a moment to relax. Allow your thoughts and feelings to take you deeper into a meditative state. Focus feelings of light and love into your Heart Chakra. Open your heart to this healing energy and allow your higher self to ask the following questions:

What does your heart want to say to you after this trip? What is your heart's unconditional message of love to you?

_____
_____
_____

RECAPPING YOUR MIND

Our brain is more than just the engine that drives us. Remember, our brain is also a conduit to a much larger collective consciousness that I call our Universal Mind. It takes a little practice each day to deliberately direct our thoughts and feelings to higher frequencies. Once we do, we can feel the power of intentionally harnessing our Universal Mind to create a better life.

Again, take a moment. Relax. Allow your feelings to become meditative. Send healing thoughts deep into your mind's expanded consciousness. Open your mind to these hi-frequency thoughts, and ask yourself:

What message does your beautiful mind want to share with you?

_____
_____
_____

RECAPPING YOUR SOUL

Remember, our soul is unconditional love personified, it's the invisible energy living inside and outside of our bodies, eternally guiding us. At the end of our lives, when we leave these bodies, we will re-emerge back into our soul's light. Once there, we will still have many of the focused nonphysical attributes we had while on Earth.

Relax. Breathe. Allow your feelings to move you even deeper into a meditative state. At this time, send light and love deep into your soul's essence.

While in this relaxed mode, ask your soul to please step forth into the light and share its message with you at this time.

_____
_____
_____

RECAPPING YOUR WITH YOUR WHOLE BEING

We always know when our heart, mind and soul trinity are blended as one, because we automatically feel absolute passion, happiness and excitement.

It's been my experience that our heart, mind and soul each carry different feeling frequencies. Our heart carries feelings that are different from our mind and soul. We must learn to relax into the unconditional love that composes our heart, mind, and soul. Remember, these aspects of our earthly experiences are already pure, positive energy. All we have to do is tap into them.

In one word, my heart feels _____

In one word, my mind feels _____

In one word, my soul feels _____

In Oneness, my heart, mind, and soul are saying, _____

A SINCERE THANK YOU

Machu Picchu

The Great Wall of China

Chichen Itza

Taj Mahal

Stonehenge

Petra Jordan

I hope you had as much fun using this Travel Journal as I did putting it together. For me, traveling is a way I consciously connect with my heart, mind, and soul while meeting new people, sharing unique experiences, and making new friendships along the way.

As a gift of appreciation for your purchase of, *"How to Get Your Travel Freq On,"* I've added two chapters from my upcoming book, *"Memoirs of A Southern Psychic – Ghosts, Angels, and Other Deep-Fried Miracles."*

Thank you again.

Until we meet again be sure to keep your thoughts, feelings, and frequencies, high, fast, and pure so that you can unlock the Universe within.

Eddie Conner is a Radio Host, Author, Humorist, Soul Intuitive, Keynote Speaker, and the Creator of Meta-Fun-ics, *Making Metaphysics Fun.*

Eddie has appeared on *America's Best TV Show, The Morning Show,* Australia, *John Edward's InfiniteQuest.com, CNN.com, Associated Press, Coast-to-Coast with George Noory,* and featured in *CBSLocal.com* for their, *Best Psychics and Mediums in Los Angeles* issue.

Eddie's Soul Intuitive abilities naturally led him to hosting shows for *CRN Radio, KIEV AM-FM, LA Talk Radio, Global Voice Broadcasting Radio, and UBN Radio* where he co-hosts, *Truth Be Told with Tony & Eddie,* doing celebrity interviews and also hosting, *Girl Your Soul is Speaking, Unlock the Universe Within,* and *Sound Bites for the Soul* segments.

An accomplished seminar leader and co-founder of, *Sail into Your Soul — A Journey into Bliss,* Eddie leads world tours and spiritual travel adventures to the Far East, The Mexican Rivera, Alaska, Hawaii, Machu Picchu, Peru, Ireland, Aruba, and more.

Eddie is amazing at elevating television, radio, and seminar audiences higher into the rich world of his BUT-Free Living principles, trademarked language, and leading edge methodologies.

Learn more at: EddieConner.com

Eddie Conner / Soul Awareness
3940 Laurel Canyon Blvd #138
Studio City, CA USA 91604

Memoirs of A Southern Psychic
Ghosts, Angels, and Other Deep-Fried Miracles

Memoirs of A Southern Psychic
Ghosts, Angels, and Other Deep-Fried Miracles

Prologue

1981   High Point, North Carolina

The afternoon a speeding car slammed into my borrowed station wagon, crashing it into a utility pole, I had recently graduated high school, was in a bad relationship, working two jobs, and babysitting to earn gas money.

Just before impact, the world around me entered a state of slow motion, like in a dream. I was pulled high above my body and into a surreal consciousness.

From overhead I watched another car T-bone mine, crushing both cars into a pile of screeching, mangled wreckage. Moving further skyward I noticed my busted windows splintering across the streets, reflecting tiny diamonds of light within the shards. It was at that moment, when the glass sparkles detonated that I realized I no longer felt a connection to my body. Every sound and earthly feeling disappeared far below while I was swept further upward.

It's true what people say about near death experiences – your life flashes before your eyes and the light wraps you inside its refuge, away from pain. I floated there while buried memories of my early life blazed before me in an odd series of rapid flashbacks:

- Me playing with my twin sister who no one else could see.

- Dad beating my pregnant Momma in front of me.

- Grandma doing an exorcism to clear me of demons she claimed had possessed me.

- Dad yelling, shaking me at his eye level before launching me against a wall.

- The ghost on Grandma's porch who disappeared into thin air seconds before I touched him.

- The first time I saw angels.

This final memory gave way to every psychic recollection and angelic visitation I'd ever had, until each experience funneled into a reflective reservoir within me.

As I watched my child self talking to my angels, I heard in the distance below me ambulance sirens and police radios. I felt chaos boiling around me, and my astral body grew dim. I remember thinking that I didn't want the light to leave me behind as it had many times before. Suddenly I was dropped from blissful perfection and back into a battered, leaden body.

I gasped, "The kids! The kids!"

As paramedics loaded me into an ambulance a fireman said, "There were not any kids in the car."

Thank God, because I had specifically borrowed the station wagon to pick up the four little munchkins I was babysitting that afternoon. I had it in my mind they were with me. Thankfully they were not.

I was released from the emergency room that night, then, against my better judgment, ended up with my lover, Lee, at Godfather's Pizza on North Main. My head, neck and back were in severe pain but I had to pretend to feel okay, because Lee wanted to do something besides sit at home and watch me recuperate. While waiting for our pizza, Lee kept feeding quarters into the Pac Man machine and drinking draft beer. I went to the men's room to decompress. Once alone in the stall, I realized it was the first time I'd been by myself in weeks, and it was a relief. I was able to quiet my mind and recall my earlier experience.

My first significant observation was that while I was in the light, I hadn't experienced myself as the insecure kid everyone had bullied and made fun of. I wasn't a victim of poverty and negative self-image, nor did I feel the typical desire to try and fit in with the crowds that had made my adolescent life a living hell.

Then it hit me; over the years I had purposely suppressed my sensitive, artistic and intuitive skills, and was taught to believe these qualities made me weak and sissified. I'd withdrawn and buried my gifts.

In the light I wasn't broken. From its expansive perspective I recognized that my childhood desires and questions were not in vain, then understood my hardships were essentially thousands of blessings.

"But, what's my purpose?" I thought.

A commode flushed in an adjoining stall.

"Wow, I hope that's not a sign."

The contrast between how I perceived myself in the light versus how I felt in everyday life was staggering. Had I unconsciously thought of myself as a victim of circumstances? Had my belief of having no self worth finally led to withering in despair over the years? The thought made me shiver.

As a child, I'd seen the light before, because that was how my angels always entered my room. Having freshly reemerged from this illuminated environment hours earlier, I had the distinct understanding that the person I was in the light was also the person I had the potential to be every day – if I chose it.

Something else peculiar happened during my time out-of-body. I had felt compassion and love for my dad, step-father, and my grandma during my flashbacks. While suspended above the wreck I didn't judge or blame them, but once I reentered my body the hurt and anger I'd harbored for them clouded my thoughts once again.

In essence, I learned happiness is ours for the taking, but we have to do something to create it for ourselves. I certainly wasn't happy. I'd stayed in a miserable relationship far too long with Lee, constantly forgetting that it takes two healthy people to make a couple work.

I enjoyed my co-workers, but hated my dead-end jobs, which didn't inspire intuition or creativity. The fact was, I'd been fed up for a couple of years, settling for the minimum wage paychecks that the world of textile mills, babysitting, and fast food had meagerly provided.

Because of the car accident I was able to revisit my true essence; a miraculous experience. As a result, I made a deliberate choice to be happy and do what I loved. This thought made me feel light again. I smiled, excited to start utilizing my strengths. I'd always wanted to uplift others in a fun, intuitive way, and after the day I'd had, I figured today was the perfect day to start.

I felt Lee's impatience pulling my attention back to the restaurant. I flushed the toilet, and washed my hands. Then, inside the men's restroom, I made a silent vow that come hell or high water, I'd figure out what my true purpose was and be happy doing what I loved, even if it killed me.

That night I barely slept. Images of the accident replayed in my mind. Each time I almost fell asleep another memory broke through as though I was swimming in calm, warm waters filled with intuitive treasures from my childhood.

Finally, I got up, grabbed my pen and journal. I decided that if I was going to gain clarity on what had happened I'd have to go back 20 years to understand my angels, the light, and other out-of-body experiences I'd had growing up.

I leaned back in my chair, careful not to strain my neck and back. "Wow," I thought, "I can't believe I remembered my angels."

I wrote, "High Point, N.C." and "1963-64" in my journal, then closed my eyes. Being a simple southern boy, I wanted to go back to the very beginning and lasso every single ghost, angel, and deep-fried miracle.

Eddie, Age 5

Memoirs of A Southern Psychic
Ghosts, Angels & Other Deep-Fried Miracles
Chapter 1

High Point, North Carolina 1963 - 64

Grandma was a strong, spirited lumberjack of a woman with a booming voice and wicked backhand that could sting your face for hours. After braiding her long, gray hair, she knotted it up in a scarf around her head that matched her imitation pearl cat-eyeglasses. Her clothes were fabric scraps she hand-sewed into a hodgepodge of garments that loosely covered her ample frame. Other accessories included yard shoes with toe holes, her butterbean gardening hat, and a set of chipped dentures her dog had gotten ahold of, leaving them riddled with canine teeth marks and one less tooth for Grandma.

Grandma rented an old, rundown property off Highway 62, surrounded by oak trees and thousands of flowers, plants, and creeping ivy vines. Over time, her house reminded me of the old witch's place in the Hansel and Gretel story, minus the cookies and candy. The first thing you felt when approaching were thick waves of suffocating heat smacking the life from your body.

Walking through her front door, your breath and sight were pinched off by unseen forces. Her two wood-burning stoves stole your breath first, followed by temporary blindness brought on by soot-covered walls, grimy pictures and second-hand furniture. Once your eyes adjusted to the dark, closed-in space, dozens of filmy pictures of Jesus watched your every move.

Everywhere you looked, there was Jesus on a cross, Jesus wearing a crown of thorns, or bloody Jesus expressing agony. There was only one serene Jesus image imprisoned inside a tarnished, ornate gold frame with a built-in tube light that accentuated his face. Any remaining wall space was peppered with decorative crosses, photos of her grandkids, lacquered biblical quotes, and angelic pictures.

Once inside, the sounds of traffic zipping along the highway mixed with firewood popping in the stove's steel stomach, as food boiled, fried, simmered or baked. From her bedroom blared a preacher's words struggling past the static of a choppy AM radio signal. The sermon was often followed by an elderly white gospel choir whose droning sounded more like dying cows in a hailstorm than the intended heavenly message.

"Children are to be seen, not heard," Grandma preached. "Don't speak unless you're spoken to." I had learned the hard way that her rules changed faster than Dad's moods, and going against her orders often meant a severe beating, or worse.

On this particular visit I was two years old and Bobby was an infant, when Momma took us to visit Grandma. Bobby slept between propped up pillows in the living room while Momma and I sat in Grandma's hot, muggy kitchen.

The small kitchen was stuffed with a faded refrigerator, huge deep-freezer, wood stove, and a homemade countertop, with plastic tubs for washing dishes with well water. The table and chairs were pushed flush against stained walls, and every surface was covered with heaps of canned goods, old bakery products, paper bags, pie tins and cooking utensils.

Momma fanned her blouse to generate cool air, when Grandma gave me a block of wood to play with. For some reason I threw it on the floor. Infuriated, Grandma popped me hard, then sharply jammed the block back into my hands. Crying, I dropped it, and with my arms held high I reached for Momma to hold me.

Grandma took ahold of my shirt, spun me around, and spanked my rear end. While hitting me she looked Momma square in the face and said, "Now you whip him too."

Instinctively, Momma pulled me back into her arms. Assuming Momma had misunderstood her, Grandma repeated, "I told you to whip him; not fuss over him!"

Teetering on the double-edged sword of being Grandma's middle daughter of thirteen children, and a teenage mother to me, Momma tried to sound respectful while standing her ground.

"No ma'am, I'm not going to hit him."

Grandma wiped sweat from her brow with the back of her hand then dried it on her apron. "What?" she shrieked, while retrieving the wooden block again.

Momma watched her in vain. "He doesn't understand why you're whipping him."

Ignoring Momma's protest, Grandma jabbed the block at me a third time. Balling my hands beneath my chin I plastered my body against Momma so Grandma couldn't reach my hind-end. Aggravated, she chunked the wood behind the stove and then spanked my bare legs harder. I cried louder. Momma stood up, grabbed Grandma's blistering hands, and when that didn't work, Momma pushed her away from me.

"Stop it," Momma said clenching her jaw, her body shielding me as Grandma swatted around Momma's hands to reach me. "I said, STOP IT!"

Grandma took a step back, and sent her daughter through seven circles of hell with her gaze. "What did you say to me?"

Pulling sweat soaked hair off her neck and flipping it over her shoulders Momma stood up, out of breath. "He didn't do anything wrong."

Grandma advanced, her voice matching the stove's overpowering heat. "You don't understand do you? You've got to break his spirit now or he'll run you for the rest of your life!"

Her words stunned Momma. Neither of them spoke for the longest time. Finally, Grandma turned her back to us, pretending to wash dishes in water she'd been boiling on the stove.

Momma gathered up our things, wrapped Bobby in a blanket, and walked us back into the cramped kitchen to say goodbye and thank Grandma for the fatback biscuits and sweet tea. We walked through the Jesus gallery to the porch. I quietly closed the screen door while Momma situated, Bobby, his things, and her pocketbook.

That's when I saw a thin, wispy image of a man's face, suspended in midair, watching us.

I closed my eyes then rubbed them open, but the man's face had already vanished. Momma took my hand again. I glanced back over my shoulder as we left the porch, in case the man's face was still there. But he was gone.

I was confused about why Grandma had whipped me. After that day I grew more afraid of her ever-changing moods, which put her in the same no-win category as my Daddy.

Playing back the incident, I knew it had taken all Momma's nerve to stand up to Grandma, but my young mind still couldn't make sense of grown-ups. As we walked to the bus stop that afternoon, Momma's hand had eventually stopped shaking and I remember glancing up to see her face, trying to imagine what she might be thinking. Though she looked straight ahead, her face unreadable to the outside world, I knew she was hurting inside but she never mentioned the incident with Grandma again. Neither did I.

I hungered to understand why bad things happened to people I loved, and why people I loved treated each other so badly. I knew Daddy loved Momma, but back then I couldn't make sense out of him beating her or us. And then there was Grandma's unpredictable craziness, all in the name of God. When she got on a roll, it seemed everyone feared her and nobody escaped her temper.

Every night I'd secretly pray and ask for help to understand what made people happy, what made them sad, and how I might help them. I figured that once I got acceptable answers, I might understand how to turn a lot of these bad family experiences into something shiny and new again, especially for Momma.

After we got home, I thought about the eerie, cloudy face that had been watching us on Grandma's porch. Misty and vapor-like, he had floated from nowhere before disappearing into thin air. I'd never seen anything like it. It made me feel strange and uncomfortable, like I wasn't allowed to be there. I wondered if the wispy face would return.

Eddie, Age 6

www.ingramcontent.com/pod-product-compliance
Lightning Source LLC
Chambersburg PA
CBHW060455300426
44113CB00016B/2604